SOMEDAY
You'll Be a GOOD
PREACHER

A Homiletical Memoir

STAN· MAST

Someday You'll Be a Good Preacher

© Stanley Mast

All Rights Reserved
Scripture quotations are taken from the *New International Study Bible*
© 1985 by The Zondervan Corporation.

Published by
Deep River Books
Sisters, Oregon
http://www.deepriverbooks.com/

ISBN: 1-935265-32-6
ISBN: 978-1-935265-32-0

Library of Congress Control Number: 2010928020

Printed in the USA

Cover Design by Robin Black

TABLE OF CONTENTS

ACKNOWLEDGMENTS

You will hear me say throughout this book that my wife has always been my strongest supporter and my sharpest critic. Sharon will brook no criticism of me, nor will she brook any nonsense from me. I would not be the person or the preacher I am today without her unswerving love and her unsparing honesty. This book would never have happened if she hadn't been with me every step of the journey to homiletical and human growth. She has been the chief means of grace in my life and growth in my ministry. I cannot thank or love her enough.

I would also like to thank all those patient and loving folks who suffered through many a sermon that fell far short of the glory of God and the good of the congregants. Without your loving support, I would have quit preaching long ago and become a high school teacher, or a real-estate agent, or best of all, a car salesman. And I need to thank all those sharp-tongued critics who pierced my delusions of preaching grandeur and by force of hard truth made me into a better preacher. I didn't always like you back then, but you were a significant part of the journey. And so were the mentors named in this slim volume. Your expert advice and instant availability saved me from many a gaffe that might have ruined me.

This book would not have been published without the encouragement and assistance of the Center for Excellence in Preaching (CEP) at Calvin Theological Seminary and the Calvin Institute of Christian Worship (CICW) at Calvin College. Rev. Scott Hoezee, the prolific director of CEP, always believed my experience was worth sharing and has unstintingly promoted my book. Dr. John Witvliet of CICW came alongside Scott in helping me get this book to press. To both of them I owe a hearty thanks.

Finally, I must thank my wonderful congregation at the LaGrave Avenue Christian Reformed Church in Grand Rapids, Michigan, for giving me sabbatical time to relive my preaching journey, collect my thoughts, and put them on paper. Your warm support and frequent praise have made these last twenty years the best part of the trip. I only hope that you have been as blessed by my preaching as I have been by your approval. Perhaps, because of you, someday I'll be a good preacher.

FOREWORD

Prior to coming to Calvin Theological Seminary in the summer of 2005, I spent just over fifteen years writing and delivering two sermons almost every week. Across those years I preached just shy of a thousand different sermons. When I took the opportunity to teach some preaching courses at Calvin—and so began to have focused conversations with students and colleagues about the preaching craft—I realized that, by sheer dint of having been doing it for a while, I knew more about preaching than I realized. I might not have been as current on formal homiletical theory or the latest articles for the guild as others were, but those years in the pulpit had provided plenty of grist for the homiletical mill.

Stan Mast discovered this same truth in his own life once he took a sabbatical opportunity to reflect on all he had learned along the way as a preacher of God's Word. Across the years of his ministry and in the varied congregations in which Stan ministered, he compiled vast tracks of insight into preaching. Stan learned, among other things, that the acoustics of the specific congregation play a mighty role in how any sermon is heard and received. He discerned a good many truths about his own self as he encountered comments and criticisms, even as those same exchanges taught him a thing or two about the hearts of God's people—the very same hearts into which preachers labor week after week to pour the content of God's gospel message.

The book in your hands is the result of Stan's reflections and reminiscences. Stan has crafted a preaching memoir that is both winsome and challenging. Experienced preachers will find in these chapters occasion to reflect back on their own life's work in the pulpit and so find cause to praise God for what he has done (and maybe even for those moments that hurt so much at the time but bore wonderful homiletical fruit later in life). Newly minted preachers will spy some sneak previews here of what lies ahead, even as they glean lessons that may begin to make them good preachers—a touch sooner, perhaps, than the "someday" of the book's title.

I am grateful to Stan Mast for having written this good book. Since Stan played an important and eminently helpful role in my own homiletical education when he worked as an assistant instructor at Calvin Theological Seminary in the mid-1980s, it gives me added pleasure to help get the ideas and memories contained in this book in front of readers.

The Center for Excellence in Preaching at Calvin Theological Seminary is dedicated to encouraging busy preachers in their vital task by providing as many good resources as we can. *Someday You'll Be a Good Preacher* most certainly counts as among the finer of those resources. May it be a blessing to all who read it.

Scott Hoezee
Director, The Center for Excellence in Preaching

INTRODUCTION

"On the road again, can't wait to get on the road again."

WILLIE NELSON

They all meant well, but I *hated* them anyway. Well, not hated exactly. Actually, it wasn't hate I felt at all. It was, rather, whatever you feel when you've been deeply hurt by someone you thought was on your side. They were trying to be nice, all of them, every well-intentioned parishioner and sharp-eyed elder, every staff member and retired minister, every idealistic teenager and battle-scarred veteran of the worship wars. But only later—much later—did I appreciate the left-handed compliments and helpful advice they dropped on my overly sensitive preacher's soul.

It started when I was young and a great preacher. I was a student at Calvin Theological Seminary. Located in Grand Rapids, Michigan, the "Jerusalem" of my lifelong denomination, the Christian Reformed Church, Calvin is a fine school in the Reformed tradition. In my day, it specialized in a rigorous classical theological education designed to produce theologically articulate preachers. (It still does, but the school has now rounded out its training to include the practical skills of ministry as well as the spiritual formation of ministers.)

Back in the late 1960s and early '70s, Calvin taught me to dig into the Bible using the universally accepted hermeneutical tools of the grammatical-historical approach, combined with the more specifically

Reformed perspective of redemptive-historical exegesis. In other words, we studied the words in the original languages, paid careful attention to the historical context in which they were written, and tried to figure out where a particular text fit into the whole flow of God's redemptive activity, especially as that activity came to its climax in the life, death, and resurrection of Jesus Christ. Then we translated the truth so mined into sermons that "reconstructed" the text in sermonic form so that the listeners could understand and apply that text in contemporary ways. This time-honored method was designed to produce sermons that were biblically shaped, theologically correct, and, at least theoretically, relevant to real life.

Having presumably mastered those basics, this twenty-five-year-old seminarian was ready to move the world with his words. Since I had been successful, at least in my own mind, at almost everything else I'd ever tried to do (baseball being the glaring and mysterious exception), I was confident that I would be a great preacher. Pouring my fine education, careful preparation, youthful energy, assumed creativity, supreme self-confidence, and Christian commitment into those fledgling sermons, I was convinced that I had nailed each one of them.

It wasn't until years later that I realized the depth of Chrysostom's wisdom when he was asked, "What is the cardinal Christian virtue?" He replied, "Humility." His interrogator then asked, "What is the second cardinal virtue?" He answered with the same word, "Humility." When his somewhat exasperated questioner asked about the third, he intoned the same thing: "Humility." Now I realize the same is true for preachers, maybe for preachers above all—but I was too naïve to know that back then.

But I'm years ahead of myself. I was preaching those fabulous sermons as a young seminarian, a veritable latter-day Spurgeon. And that's when it started. A little old lady would shake my hand at the door after a service. Or a middle-aged elder would catch me in the council room as I gathered my belongings. Or a little knot of people chatting in the narthex, having a little roast preacher with their coffee, would toss off their comment as I walked by. One after another, these good folks would say it, intending to be helpful, trying to encourage a novice: "Someday you'll be a good preacher."

"Thank you," I would say aloud, with my best false modesty. *What do you mean, someday?* I would murmur in my arrogant young mind. *Someday is already here!* I really thought I had arrived as a preacher, when those experienced pew-sitters knew the train hadn't even left the station. They could see that I was just purchasing my ticket to preaching places unknown, and they were eager to give me directions because they had already travelled to those places with far more experienced preachers than I. They meant well, but I felt—not hate—hurt, shock, offense, wounded pride. In other words, exactly what the Master Preacher ordered for this strutting neophyte.

Thus began the journey that has finally led to the writing of this slender volume. You need to know up front that I don't think *someday* has arrived yet. I'm a much better preacher today than I was back when I knew it all. In fact, I'm tempted to say in moments of weakness and folly that I am a good preacher, except for a recurring experience on the twisting mountain highway on which I have been traveling for nearly four decades.

My formative years were spent in Denver, Colorado. I was raised there back in the days when the air was so pure and the high-rise apartments so rare that I could see the famous Red Rocks Amphitheater from my kitchen window, even though it was some twenty miles away. I can't begin to count the number of trips my family took up those winding mountain roads to our favorite fishing spots. Though I currently live in the relative flatlands of Michigan, I was recently reminded of the phenomenon of mountain travel as my wife and I drove to Aspen, Colorado, where I sketched the rough draft of this book. Interstate 70 and then Colorado 82 presented us with one breathtaking discovery after another.

When you're traveling on a mountain highway, you never know what the next turn will present to your eyes. It might be a rugged snow-covered peak or a mighty river roaring through a deep canyon, nearly ominous in its high-walled grandeur; it might a valley meadow filled with impossibly brilliant wildflowers, a little mountain brook tumbling alongside the road, or astonishingly elegant luxury condominiums built right next to dilapidated old cabins. With every turn in the road, there is a new vista, a new perspective, a new discovery.

So it has been with the mountain road on which I have traveled as a preacher. I have at times allowed myself to say, "I'm here. I've arrived. I am a good preacher now." Then I turn a corner on the road to excellence and discover a whole new vista, a different perspective than I have ever seen before—a new issue, a different question, a fresh insight, a novel approach. And I realize that *someday* is not here yet.

I write this book as a record of those several turns in the hope that my experience will encourage my fellow preacher, whether callow novice, struggling apprentice, skilled journeyman, or master pulpiteer. I make no claim to writing the metanarrative that will definitively prescribe how others should proceed down the road to their own *someday.* This is simply my own story, my own *petite narrative,* as postmodern thinkers like to say. In fact, my narrative may be more petite than most, since I come from the unique, in some ways peculiar, little Dutch Reformed subculture called the Christian Reformed Church. What I tell you here is not intended to be prescriptive, merely descriptive.

My hopes for this book are modest. I want to encourage preachers and those who long for good preaching. Perhaps my journey can help new seminarians and preachers in their first churches. I would be delighted if something in my experience prepared another for those ego-deflating but ultimately uplifting experiences that will come every preacher's way, so that those experiences will produce growth rather than death in a young preacher. Or perhaps this memoir will enable some old pros to relive their journey and finally thank God for those awkward, disappointing, sometimes excruciatingly painful moments when someone suggests non-too-gently that the preacher in front of him needs to get a lot better before anyone will say, "Now you are a good preacher." At the very least, I hope my story will evoke a smile of recognition from those who have traveled the same road and learned the same lessons.

I wish I could tell you that I've learned all my lessons from my teachers, from those experts with their elaborate homiletical maps pointing the way to good preaching with unerring accuracy. And of course, I have learned much from the professionals who have taught me. In fact, I encourage all preachers, wherever they are on the journey, to keep reading books about preaching and listening to the great preachers around them. These experts have taught me much.

Some of my best teachers, however, have been not only rank amateurs, but also rapier-tongued critics. Throughout this book I've used the real names of the professionals, because they are accustomed to being public figures, and anyone who wants to could discover who they are anyway. However, I've changed the names of my lay critics, because they all meant well, and I don't want anyone to criticize them for the hard things they said to me. The last thing I want to do is embarrass those good folks who helped me make progress on this long mountain road that will hopefully lead me, someday, to being a good preacher.

When I told my wife about the general thrust of this book and particularly my intention to feature my critics, she wondered aloud about the wisdom of it. "Why wouldn't you include all of your supporters? Why wouldn't you mention so-and-so?" She instantly rattled off the names of a dozen who had loved us and lifted us when times were tough, and then added another dozen who through their generosity and kindness had simply made life more pleasant. "We couldn't have made it without those supporters!" And, of course, she was right. Those folks who never said a discouraging word, who extended themselves sacrificially to fill our lives with grace and peace, were the human bedrock of our survival and growth as human beings and as Christians. Without them, the critics would have killed me as a preacher. I would have simply quit and gone back to what I wanted to do with my life in the first place. I'll never be able to thank all those lovely folks enough. Without all of you, I wouldn't be in ministry today. But the fact remains that it was the critics who moved me to change as a preacher.

That, perhaps, is my fondest hope for this little book—that preachers will not only appreciate their supporters, but also learn from their critics. Conversely, I hope that those critics will realize how powerful their words can be—for good and for ill. (Remember, without all those cheerleaders on my side, the words of the critics would have driven me out of the pulpit.) I have learned much from my critics. That doesn't mean I've always liked them. Indeed, when I'm criticized today, I still wrestle with that old reptilian response to pain—fight or flight. But when I've listened and learned, these critics have forced me to navigate turns on the mountain road, and I've discovered new vistas on preaching that I never suspected were there. With words I never wanted to hear, they moved me from my supposed present excellence to another leg of the journey.

That grizzled old country singer Willie Nelson sings about the journey of life in his nasal twang, "On the road again, can't wait to get on the road again." The premise of this book, the experience of my preaching life, is that if you are willing to get on the road again and again, and not just set your heels and settle into what you've always done but be willing to learn from your strongest amateur critics as well as your professional superiors, then someday you'll be a good preacher.

Chapter One

CALL

"Lord, please send someone else to do it."

EXODUS 4:13

W hen writer Lynn Freed implored a Japanese piano teacher to take her seven-year-old daughter as a student, the teacher said she didn't teach Caucasian children because they lacked dedication. For that matter, she didn't teach Japanese children either. She taught only Chinese children, because she said they understood excellence. But Freed persisted, the teacher relented, and for seven years Freed's daughter took lessons from this instructor, learning to make the most of her abilities. Despite the daughter's success, as a teenager she rebelled against the discipline of lessons and practice. Freed concluded that although her daughter "had a nice touch and a passable technique, she lacked what is essential in any art: a vocation."[1]

The same is true for preachers. No one can even begin the journey to becoming a good preacher without a vocation, a call from God. Oh yes, one might become a fine orator, a pleasing public speaker, an effective communicator without a call from God. But without a divine vocation, even the most gifted speaker cannot become a preacher of God's Word. I surely couldn't. Indeed, I would never have taken one step on my winding journey had I not been called to preach by God.

THE CALL TO LEAVE

Like Abraham of old, my journey began with a call to leave what I knew and loved and go to something I didn't know or want. I suspect that's always how it goes. I understand Abraham's story to be archetypal; he was, after all, the father of all believers. The journey of faith that took that wandering Aramean all over the Middle East began with the famous call: "Leave your country, your people and your father's household and go to a land I will show you." And the famous response: "So Abram left, as the Lord had told him" (Genesis 12:1, 4).

Hundreds of years later, the letter to the Hebrews summed up that seminal event in the history of salvation with words designed to encourage all of God's children to walk by faith. "By faith Abraham, when he was called to go to a place he would later receive as his inheritance, obeyed and went, even though he did not know where he was going" (Hebrews 11:8). So it began—it all began: the story of Abraham, the story of Israel, the story of redemption, the story of my own journey. It all began with God's call to leave and go. You can't be a follower of Christ, let alone a preacher of the Christian gospel, without such a call.

If you think I've said that too strongly, consider the stories of famous biblical preachers. Take, for example, the story of Moses, the quintessential prophet of the Old Testament. Though always identified as a mighty leader, he was first of all a great prophet. Indeed, he was such a powerful prophet that he became a type of the coming Messiah. He said, "The Lord your God will raise up for you a prophet like me from among your own brothers" (Deuteronomy 18:15, cf. Acts. 7:37). When the crowds milling around Jesus tried to figure out who he was, some wondered if Jesus might be, at last, the great prophet predicted by Moses (John 6:14).

I find it helpful that Moses didn't want to be a prophet any more than I wanted to be a preacher. When God called him, he wasn't thinking about leading God's people with a powerful word from God. He was thinking about leading his father-in-law's sheep to pasture in the wilderness near Mt. Horeb, the mountain of God. He knew that life;

he'd been at it for forty years. But then he was distracted from his cho-
sen path by a strange sight, a bush ablaze with God. After scaring Moses
half to death by introducing himself as the God of his fathers, God told
Moses that he had heard the cries of his children suffering under
Pharaoh. Without further ado, God called and sent Moses on a mission:
"So now, go. I am sending you to Pharaoh to bring my people the
Israelites out of Egypt" (Exodus 3:10).

Rather than being thrilled with such a calling, Moses filled the air
with his reluctance. "What should I tell them when they ask me who
sent me? What if they don't believe me or want to listen to me?" (Exodus 3:13–14). Those are bedrock questions that every preacher ought
to ponder before beginning the journey. But even when God answered
them, Moses had one more problem with his call: "O Lord, I have never
been eloquent, neither in the past nor since you have spoken to your
servant. I am slow of speech and tongue" (Exodus 4:10).

God's reply is the ultimate comfort for every self-doubting
preacher. "Who gave man his mouth? Is it not I, the Lord? Now go. I
will help you speak and will teach you what to say." Moses then spoke
for every foot-dragger like me. "O Lord, please send someone else to
do it." Even when Moses persisted in his terrified reluctance, God
pressed his call upon the man whose prophetic ministry would fore-
shadow the Christ. (You'll find this part of the story in Exodus
4:11–12.)

It is fascinating and comforting to note that other great prophets
responded to God's call as Moses did, with a reluctance born of doubt
and a sense of inadequacy. Think of Isaiah. Like Moses, his vocation
began with a personal encounter with God. In Isaiah's case, it wasn't a
burning bush. It was a vision of God's holiness so overpowering that
Isaiah cried out, "Woe is me! I am ruined! For I am a man of unclean
lips…and my eyes have seen the King, the Lord Almighty" (Isaiah 6:5).
God responded to Isaiah's sense of sin with a blazing grace. Touching
Isaiah's lips with a live coal taken from the altar that burned before the
thrice-Holy One, a seraph said, "See, this has touched your lips; your
guilt is taken away and your sin atoned for" (Isaiah 6:7). Those words

and that symbolic action not only took away Isaiah's guilt, but also purified his lips for the ministry that would soon begin.

Immediately, God calls. "Then I heard the voice of the Lord saying, 'Whom shall I send? And who will go for us?'" Isaiah answers with equal immediacy. "Here I am. Send me" (Isaiah 6:8). Now, that was much smoother than the call of Moses, but if you think Moses had reason to hesitate, consider the kind of ministry to which God called Isaiah! God told Isaiah bluntly that the people would not listen to him. In fact, there was a sense in which his unwelcome preaching was to be part of God's judgment on them. That unfruitful ministry would go on, said God, "until the cities lie ruined and without inhabitant...until the Lord has sent everyone away" (Isaiah 6:11–12). No one could stick with a preaching ministry like that unless God had called him to it.

It was the same with Jeremiah. In words that anticipate Paul's sense of predestination, God introduced himself to Jeremiah. "Before I formed you in the womb I knew you, before you were born I set you apart. I appointed you as a prophet [literally, "as one who had been called"] to the nations" (Jeremiah 1:5). You would think that Jeremiah would have been on fire to preach after such a call, but he responds, like Moses and Isaiah, with a protest about his inadequacy. "Ah, Sovereign Lord...I do not know how to speak; I am only a child" (Jeremiah 1:6). Compare this with Solomon's words in I Kings 3:7, and you'll learn that Jeremiah was no older than twenty, a callow youth like you-know-who.

God doesn't care about such things:

"Do not say, 'I am only a child.' You must go to everyone I send you to and say whatever I command you. Do not be afraid of them, for I am with you and will rescue you," declares the Lord. Then the Lord reached out his hand and touched my mouth and said to me, "Now I have put my words in your mouth. See, today I appoint you over nations and kingdoms to uproot and tear down, to destroy and overthrow, to build and to plant." (Jeremiah 1:7, 9–10)

To survive a ministry like that, Jeremiah needed this direct and specific call from God.

Finally, perhaps the least auspicious beginning to a preaching ministry was that of Saul the Pharisee. After the martyrdom of Stephen, says Acts 8:3, "Saul began to destroy the church. Going from house to house, he dragged off men and women and put them in prison." Not content to persecute Christians in Jerusalem, Paul sought permission to pursue those Christians fleeing that persecution as far away as Damascus.

But, goes the now-familiar story, God had another idea for this persecuting Pharisee. He would make him a preacher. As with Moses, Isaiah, and Jeremiah, Paul's call began with a life-changing encounter with the living God, the resurrected Christ. But Paul didn't open his mouth to preach until God called him through a member of the Damascus church. "Go!" Jesus said to the reluctant Ananias. "This man is my chosen instrument to carry my name before the Gentiles and their kings and before the people of Israel. I will show him how much he must suffer for my name" (Acts 9:15–16). As soon as he got his sight and his strength back, "Saul began to preach in the synagogue that Jesus is the Son of God" (Acts 9:20). So was unleashed a preacher who would change the world for Christ, because he had encountered that Christ and knew Christ had called him.

In Galatians 1:15, Paul summarized that call: "But when God, who set me apart from birth and called me by his grace, was pleased to reveal his Son in me that I might preach him among the Gentiles, I did not consult any man." That sense of gracious calling enabled Paul to survive all the hostility he would encounter in his ministry.

My Call

In all the stories of these great preachers, I am struck by the sheer weakness, reluctance, inadequacy, hostility, and sinfulness in them. Surely not all preachers are in this condition when God calls, but I'm glad for these stories because they resonate so strongly with God's call to me.

It was Reformation Day, October 31, 1962. America was at peace. Korea was a distant though still painful memory for some, but not for me. The disaster in Vietnam was only just beginning, and I knew almost nothing of it. I was enjoying the life of a high school junior. It was an idyllic time, at least in my memory. Genuine society-wide adolescent rebellion had not yet swept away a generation, though I do distinctly recall the first hint of that cultural tsunami as we caught our first glimpse of the Beatles on Ed Sullivan's TV show. I was happily occupied with the things I loved—sports (except baseball) and girls (one in particular).

Then came Reformation Day. In the little Dutch Reformed subculture to which I belonged, it was the custom to celebrate the day of our ecclesiastical birth with a large rally. That year it was held in the cavernous auditorium of the Denver South Public High School. The speaker was Dr. Peter Eldersveld, the riveting preacher of *The Back to God Hour,* the radio outreach ministry of the Christian Reformed Church. I was there, not because I was overly religious, but because everyone in our church community was there, especially my parents who had compelled me to go. I wasn't all that reluctant (remember, teenage rebellion hadn't really begun in earnest yet, at least not where I lived), but I cannot tell you what Dr. Eldersveld said that day. I'd guess it was about some Reformation theme. But I can tell you exactly what God said. It was about my being a preacher.

I did not want to hear that, though I had been sensing some strange spiritual stirrings for a number of months. I pushed these stirrings to the back of mind whenever they would arise because any thought of ministry placed me and my plans in mortal jeopardy. No one had ever suggested any sort of ministry to me as a vocation, but for some reason I was afraid that God would call me to mission work in Nigeria, where the CRC had a marvelous ministry. I had no desire to become a mendicant missionary far away from all I knew and loved. So I pushed those thoughts down and away and focused on the known and the loved— sports and my girlfriend. I had no plans for her, but I deeply wanted to be a high school teacher and, mostly, a coach of basketball and track.

Then came that Reformation Day and the call of God. It was so clear and powerful that I simply dropped all my objections and plans and said, "OK, I'll be a minister." That's about as dramatic as it got. I didn't see a burning bush or hear God audibly or get struck blind. There was no dramatically salacious surrendering like Anne Lamott in her *Traveling Mercies* or noble volunteering like Isaiah after he was undone by that overpowering vision. But God impressed his call on my mind in a way so unmistakable that I knew what I had to do. So, like the stolid Dutch Calvinist that I was, I bowed before the will of the sovereign God and said, "OK."

With that, I left behind what I knew and loved to go somewhere I didn't know or want. That's how my journey began, though I must tell you in all honesty that I spent the next ten years (right up to the moment I actually became a minister, and truth be told, even beyond that) trying to prove that one could be both called by God and cool in the world, both Christian preacher and worldly bon vivant, *simul justus et peccator.* But I never lost my certainty of God's call. I wouldn't be writing this if I had any doubt.

No Call, No Preacher

I'm convinced that you cannot be a preacher without a clear sense of divine vocation. It's just too hard, too demanding, too painful. I think that what God said to Paul through Ananias back in Acts 9 is true for every preacher: "I will show him how much he will suffer for my name." Much later, Paul summarized his ministry with those words in II Corinthians 4:8–12 that every preacher understands all too well:

> We are hard pressed on every side, but not crushed; perplexed, but not in despair; persecuted, but not abandoned; struck down, but not destroyed. We always carry around in our body the death of Jesus, so that the life of Jesus may also be revealed in our body. For we who are alive are always being given over to death for Jesus' sake, so that his life may be revealed in our

mortal body. So then, death is at work in us [preachers], but life is at work in you [Christians].

To endure as a preacher, you must be called. To grow and be a blessing to others, you must be called. That's where my journey began. It does for everyone who will someday be a good preacher.

I love the conclusion of this true story from the February 21, 2006 issue of *The Christian Century*. When Anthony Robinson asked a young seminarian how he was called to ministry, the young man confessed that he had been a teenager from hell. He started drinking in ninth grade, moving on to drugs a year or two later. He barely made it through high school and flunked out of college the first year. He was living with his girlfriend, and for some reason they started attending a small Presbyterian church. The pastor told him, "I think you would be good working with youth." She kept after him until he gave it a try. Eventually he went back to school and finished his degree while still working at the church.

One day he said to his girlfriend, "I think God is calling me to ministry." And much to his surprise, she said, "I think that's right."

So they went to his parents to tell them about this call. Upon hearing the news, his mother started to cry and said, "You don't know this, but we had a hard time conceiving a child. I had several miscarriages. One day I was at church and heard this story about Hannah and how she had trouble conceiving a child, and about how she promised that if she had a son he would be a minister. So, Sam, I did that."

Sam, now the young seminarian, said to Anthony Robinson, "That's how I got here, and I've learned never to underestimate God."[2]

Well, now you know how I got here on this long mountain road. I wish I could tell you that I've never underestimated God. But that's part of the rest of the story.

Chapter Two

TRUTH

"The times they are a-changing."

BOB DYLAN

He cocked his head ever so slightly and peered at me through thick glasses, above which twitched eyebrows as thick as wooly caterpillars. Clearing his throat in his nervous way and smiling thinly, he asked me the question that would force me to make my first sharp turn on the road to being a good preacher.

James Jones was a convert—not to Christianity, but to the Reformed version of it. Raised a Baptist, he had found his way to the Reformed faith in general and the Trinity Christian Reformed Church in particular, that little A-frame church nestled at the bottom of a bowl of low hills covered with the brand-new subdivisions of the western suburbs of St. Louis, Missouri. As with nearly all the recent converts I have met in my thirty-nine years on the road, Jim was passionate about his newfound theology.

So when I walked through the door of Trinity that summer evening in 1971, an eager and confident candidate for the position of mission-ary pastor of that tiny church, there was just one thing Jim wanted to know from me. "How would you preach Christ to a mixed congrega-tion, one in which some people are professed and genuine Christians and others are of indeterminate salvific status?" Yes, Jim actually talked that way. He worked at a local seminary and would begin his doctoral studies while I was his pastor, a move that made him even more alert to doctrinal distinctions.

I had come to St. Louis for just such questions, though not that one—surely not that contentious one in particular! Nearly a decade had passed since God had called me to be a minister, and the times had changed dramatically. The peace and prosperity of the idyllic '50s and early '60s had been shattered by Vietnam War protestors, the free love movement and its hippie prophets, and a society-wide challenging of authority that brought all previously assumed truth and morality into question.

My own life in those ten years was largely insulated from all that foment, though of course I knew about it from the media. My college years were spent on the tree-lined paths of a small conservative Reformed college in quintessentially Midwestern Grand Rapids, Michigan. Calvin College is the official college of the CRC and is firmly rooted in a Reformed world-and-life view that considers all of reality fair game for creative study and redemptive transformation. The troubled waters of American society occasionally created a ripple on our little pond, but mostly we studied and played and went to church and dated. It was during those four years that I met and married my wife, Sharon. Since we met in a freshman Latin class (she was the cute blonde two seats down my row), she has been my constant companion, fellow sufferer, and persistent teacher on the road to becoming a good preacher.

Three years at Calvin Theological Seminary followed my collegiate career, and those years were, if anything, even more placid—as undisturbed as the sheltered surface of the seminary pond over which some of us skated on frigid Michigan nights. The only overt incursion of the wider secular culture was a protest launched by Calvin College "radicals" who objected to a planned trip by the Seminary Choir, in which I sang a middling second tenor. We were invited to sing at President Nixon's White House on Mother's Day, and some college students wondered quite vociferously if that wasn't a tacit Christian baptism of the Vietnam War. We listened to them, but were unmoved. We went anyway; I still have a picture of the choir with the embattled president.

We were not exactly at the cutting edge of the protest culture.

On the other hand, in the spirit of our Reformed heritage ("a Reformed church is always reforming"), we did question our professors very sharply, challenging our centuries' old theological traditions. But in the end, I bought it all and was ready to face the world with the truth "once for all delivered to the saints," that "pattern of sound teaching" passed on from Paul to us (Jude 3 and II Timothy 1:13). As I left the safe and hallowed halls of Calvin Seminary, the words of Paul in II Timothy 1:14 seemed to me to be my marching orders: "Guard the good deposit that was entrusted to you—guard it with the help of the Holy Spirit who lives in us."

A FORK IN THE ROAD

The only question now was, which direction should I march? There was a fork in the road before me, for I had calls to two churches. One fork led to a traditional church right in Grand Rapids, where the CRC is headquartered. It was considered a real honor in those days for a seminarian to get a call to a church right in "Jerusalem." It was a healthy church of some ninety families with perhaps three hundred members. Arcadia CRC was a real plum, I thought.

The other branch led to the ends of the earth, as least as far as I was concerned. It was a little mission church in St. Louis, Missouri. Numbering about twenty-three families and less than a hundred people, it had been planted out there in the big city along the banks of the mighty Mississippi River to reach the heathen far from Jerusalem. Its little A-frame stuck out like a tiny beacon of light for the pagans living in the surrounding subdivisions, neighborhoods with names like Pheasant Run and Bluebell Hills. If Arcadia was a coveted prize, Trinity was an overwhelming challenge.

Absolutely stuck at that fork in the road, I sought the advice of a seasoned traveler. Dr. Mel Hugen had served an inner-city church in Grand Rapids during the racially charged '60s and then a mission church in Hawaii. Now he was professor of pastoral care at Calvin Seminary and widely respected for his compassion and sage advice. When

I came seeking that advice, he characteristically did not tell me what to do. But he told me of his experience out on the frontier in Hawaii.

"A mission church will force you back to basics," he said. "The sheer fact that you have to preach the gospel to those who don't know it or believe it will force you to think through the basics of the gospel in a way you probably won't have to do in an established church. An experience like St. Louis will shape the way you preach the gospel for the rest of your life. You will always preach as a missionary, asking how to make the gospel clear and relevant and persuasive to seekers and unbelievers."

That wisdom moved me to take the road less traveled, and I've never been sorry. Dr. Hugen was exactly right. Life on the frontier shaped my preaching for ever after. And that reshaping began with Jim Jones's question, a question that immediately forced me back to the basics. I knew them well, but he was asking how I would preach them to a congregation that might include unbelievers. How do you make that truth "once for all delivered," the truth I was supposed to "guard with the help of the Holy Spirit," clear and winsome to those who hear it as new and strange? It was the quintessential missionary question.

However, Jim wasn't only, or even mainly, interested in missiology. He was forcing me to confront the burning theological issue in the CRC in the tumultuous early '70s. Our storm had to do not with Vietnam or free love, but with God's love for his elect. The CRC had historically been a staunchly Calvinistic church, a Five-Point Calvinist church. For as long as I can remember, the distinctly Reformed understanding of salvation has been summarized in the acronym TULIP, which stands for Total Depravity (how bad is the condition of sinful humanity), Unconditional Election (how did salvation begin in eternity), Limited Atonement (for whom did Christ die), Irresistible Grace (how does a person become a believer), and Perseverance of the Saints (how certain is salvation once one has believed).

Jim's question grew out of a new dispute in the CRC about the U and the L. Officially and historically, we believed not only that God had chosen some for salvation while passing others by in their sin, but also that Jesus had died only for those chosen ones. So, when we preached the gospel, we always did it in the light of those pillar truths. And though such ideas horrify the majority of Christians, who are Arminians (after Jacob Arminius, the seventeenth-century Dutch theologian who challenged the prevailing Calvinism of his native land), they were not a problem for us as long as we were preaching only to believers and their (covenant) children.

Now, however, we were beginning to take our mission task more seriously. World World II had thrust many CRC folks out into the world, where contact with all kinds of people broke the insular shell of Dutch Reformed subculture. One of the CRC soldiers was a chaplain named Harold Dekker, who became a professor of missions at Calvin Seminary. He challenged the church to think more deeply about those twin pillars of Unconditional Election and Limited Atonement. Particularly, he asked if we hadn't allowed these doctrinal formulations to blur the clear biblical message of God's love for the world. And what about all those texts that seem to say, "Jesus died for all"? The CRC was in turmoil over what was called "the Dekker controversy."

That's what I walked into that early summer evening in St. Louis in the person of James Jones, convert to classical high Calvinism. He was convinced that Dekker was threatening the entire edifice of Reformed truth, and he wanted to make sure I didn't shake the foundations of that little church out there on the edge of the prairie. "How would you preach Christ to a mixed congregation?" he asked. I hadn't thought much about the Dekker controversy, so I stumbled and stammered my way around Reformed doctrine long enough to convince him for the moment that I could serve as the missionary pastor of the Trinity CRC.

THREE LONG YEARS

My wife and I left the safe Jerusalem of Grand Rapids, where she had been born twenty-five years before and where our first son, Greg, had been born nine short months ago, and traveled to the ends of the earth. We moved from a tiny upstairs apartment in an old home in the inner city of Grand Rapids to a rambling new suburban home adjacent to the church parking lot in which Greg learned to ride his little Hot Wheels tricycle at breakneck speeds. That would be our home for three long years.

I say *long* because Jim set the tone for my ministry there. At the front door, he helped me turn the first corner on my journey. I call it *the truth corner*. How do you preach the truth? It's not enough to know it well. The question is, how do you preach it in a way that both preserves and propagates the truth of the ages and takes account of the various backgrounds of the people sitting before you at the moment?

Jim helped me to become hypervigilant about the truth. Indeed, those early sermons were virtual treatises of Reformed doctrine. Oh, I tried to make them relevant. This was a mission church after all; I was supposed to bring seekers into the kingdom. But my deepest concern was to be theologically correct at all times. Even in sermons specifically designed to be evangelistic, sermons that explained the person and work of Christ in such simple terms that even a child in the faith or one not yet born in the faith could understand, sermons that ended with a specific call to be born again by repentance and faith, there was much more theological precision than spiritual passion. I was more careful to get the truth right than to get the lost saved.

After all, Jim was always out there. So was Bill Scott, a stern Scottish refugee from the Presbyterian Church and all the issues it faced in those turbulent times. He had been, in his words, "once burned," and he wasn't going to let it happen again. He was particularly prickly about anything that smacked of social gospel and vehement about anything antiwar. When I used the bombing and mining of Hanoi Harbor as an illustration in a sermon, Bill met me at the door so red-faced I thought he would have a heart attack. "Don't you ever bring that antiwar stuff in here!" he bellowed in the hearing of all one hundred worshipers. I really hadn't, but his overreaction made me ever more careful about how I worded even illustrations.

Then there was the O'Donald family, former Catholics who came into the CRC in St. Louis via the charismatic movement. David read

Calvin's *Institutes* for fun, and Jess was always praying that I'd be baptized in the Spirit. One Sunday I opened the sermon by quoting John 3:16 in Greek, Genesis 1:1 in Hebrew, and the Lord's Prayer in German. Jess's hands flew to the heavens in praise to God for the gift of speaking in tongues that had finally been given to me in answer to her many prayers.

The Petersons were Reformed Baptists, fanatically devoted to Puritan Calvinism but equally convinced that infant baptism was a fundamental misreading of Scripture. They had been excommunicated from a local Baptist church as members of "the synagogue of Satan" (Revelation 2:9) because of their persistent and voluble criticism of dispensational premillennialism. I heard from them often before they moved on to more correct pastures.

When you add in the lapsed Methodist who was now a devotee of Edgar Cayce's version of the occult, the Jehovah's Witnesses living next door, and all the neighbors who worshiped the great god of nature with their fishing rods and golf clubs, you can see why I was preoccupied with the truth issue in every single sermon.

Looking back on those days, it seems to me that some of those folks fell into the category of what Paul called "contentious" (Titus 3:10), and I should have finally tuned them out. But in God's plan for my development as a preacher, St. Louis was the place I would learn to pay careful attention to how I spoke the truth. Yes, it is possible to become overly careful and lose one's prophetic sharpness. But St. Louis taught me that I'd better be very careful that my prophetic, evangelistic sermons were pastorally sensitive (true to people), theologically correct (true to the Word), and thoughtfully articulate about the cultural ramifications of what I preached (true to the world).

It wasn't always fun in St. Louis. Being watched carefully by those perched as watchers on the walls of Zion and the target of frequent arrows from on high can be a tense and painful business. But I turned an important corner there, thanks to Jim and Bill and all the rest. Since that time, I haven't had to question the basics very often.

When I left that little church in Missouri, I thought I knew how to preach. I didn't even ask what more there could be for me to learn. I rushed out of that graduate school in theological preaching, knowing where I was going but not what I would learn there.

The road to Colorado Springs, my next stop, led straight across the prairie. I never could have guessed how the road would turn once I arrived at the foothills of the Rockies. After all, I was a good preacher now.

Chapter Three

BIBLE

"Preach the Word."

II TIMOTHY 4:1

I was absolutely delighted to receive the call to Colorado Springs. It was time to leave St. Louis, though the church did not agree. I was exhausted from all the learning! Besides being a graduate education in theological preaching, St. Louis was a postgraduate education in ministry and life. The demands of a small church (which I now know are often greater than those of a very large church), combined with our rookie naïvete, had put Sharon and me into a position where we simply needed to leave. Lacking the wisdom and courage to establish boundaries, our lives and even our home had become so intertwined with the church that we felt almost suffocated—and that by a fine little church full of good folks. I worked seventy hours a week, and since our basement had been transformed into Sunday School rooms, my downtime with family was often interrupted by people who had come to prepare their room for class on Sunday. We didn't know how to say *no* to God's people in St. Louis. So we were glad to say *yes* to God when he said, "Go west, young folks, go west."

FROM EXHAUSTING TO EXHILARATING

Besides the joy of moving out of an exhausting situation, we had the joy of moving into an exciting one. The Cragmor Christian Reformed

Church was a former mission church like St. Louis, but it had grown up and graduated to independent adulthood. Now it was a blooming, booming church. A few years before our arrival, a membership of a mere forty families had organized and run a Vacation Bible School for over eight hundred children. The church had doubled in size under the charismatic leadership of my predecessor, Rev. Wayne Leys, and then built a beautiful and functional building that featured a bright, airy sanctuary with a split chancel and multiple windows that allowed the brilliant Colorado sunshine to stream into the warm worship space. There was no sign that the growth was going to stop. Members regularly invited their neighbors to worship services and Bible studies. When those neighbors came, they often were converted and became members themselves. It was everything my missionary heart ever could have hoped for.

The icing on the cake was that I was now back home in the Rockies. Unlike Abraham, I knew where I was going when I took the call to Cragmor CRC. I knew this place and these people. They were mine. I was home. The picture window of our cozy brick home was filled with the eastern face of Pikes Peak. My wife spent many a night gazing out on that ever-changing mountain as she held our second son, Benjamin, born a year earlier in St. Louis. He was prone to ear infections and coughing fits that made lying down impossible. Sharon held him upright so he could sleep as she studied Pike's Peak. Congregants had a similar view in church, as the whole front of the building was dominated by a huge window with an awesome view of the Front Range of the Rockies. It all reminded me of Denver, which was only sixty miles to the north. I was looking forward to the relative comfort of familiar turf. Besides, I knew how to preach now.

That illusion lasted about three weeks. That's when Al Negen ushered me around the next turn in the road and showed me a whole new perspective on preaching. Actually, *ushered* isn't the right word. Al didn't usher; he bulldozed. He was a sturdy Minnesota farm boy become bristly-bearded Colorado cowboy. Occupying the position of Director of Youth and Education at Cragmor, he was my partner in minister. I liked him immediately. Always dressed in tight faded jeans and cowboy boots, Al strode into rooms and took them over, his voice booming, his pale blue eyes snapping. His ready smile, great sense of humor, and direct manner made him a joy to be around. I was looking forward to working with him for many years.

"You Don't Preach the Bible"

That's why I was simply bowled over by what Al said as he blew by me one Sunday morning after the service. As I stood there shaking hands, I thought things had gone well until Al dropped his bombshell. "You know, it sure would be nice if I needed to bring my Bible to church again!" When I looked at him in obvious confusion, he said, "You never open your Bible or make us open ours. When Wayne preached, he was all over the Book. Sometimes I tore pages trying to keep up with him. But I guess you don't preach the Bible."

I was stunned. Of course I preached the Bible. That's how I was raised. That's how I was trained. That's how I prepared sermons. I spent hours on biblical exegesis. I wholeheartedly believed Paul's famous injunction to his young pastoral protege: "In the presence of God and of Christ Jesus, who will judge the living and the dead, and in view of his appearing and his kingdom, I give you this charge: Preach the Word; be prepared in season and out of season; correct, rebuke and encourage—with great patience and careful instruction" (II Timothy 4:1–2). I *was* preaching the Word. My sermons were full of biblical truth as interpreted by the Reformed faith. That's what I had just learned to do so well back there on the banks of the Mississippi. What was that crazy cowboy talking about?

Once I got past my shock and hurt and anger, I sat down with Al to pursue the matter. It turned out that he wasn't talking as much about the substance of the message as about the style or method in which the message was delivered. Al's frame of reference was Wayne Leys, whom he loved deeply and whose departure he was still grieving. (It didn't help that I wasn't Al's first choice to be Wayne's successor. He and his wife had voted for the other guy, convinced that I wasn't the

right man for Cragmor.) Wayne's preaching style had deeply impressed
Al, and he was judging me by that standard.

In the preaching I had witnessed as a youth and was trained to do
at Calvin, the preacher would finish the reading of a text, say, "Thus
endeth the reading of God's Holy Word," (yes, preachers kept talking
that way far into the twentieth century), close the book, and then
deliver a soundly Reformed theological reconstruction of that text. The
Word was preached, just as Paul had commanded Timothy to do. So,
for example, I would preach a sermon on Ephesians 1:3–6 dealing with
the theology of election and predestination. After reading that text, I
would close my Bible and deliver a three-point sermon in which I dis-
cussed the biblical basis of election, the human objections to election,
and the divine response to the human objections. That was the way
the Word had been preached in the CRC for a hundred years.

But something had changed in the church and in the world in
those mid-1970s. The youth revolution of the '60s had spawned its
own revolution: the Jesus Movement, in which thousands of free-lov-
ing, pot-smoking, biblically ignorant young people fell in love with the
radical Jesus. Eventually they began to come to church, where they
needed to learn the Bible. They knew Jesus, but they didn't know the
Word. Eventually they would need theology, but first they simply
needed to know what the Bible said.

So a whole generation of Bible preachers and teachers rose up to
meet them. Bibles in hand, these preachers worked verse-by-verse
through whole chapters and books, constantly cross-referencing so that
new Christians could follow the flow of the whole Bible. There was
never any overt mention of theology, though of course they were teaching theology. Ostensibly and intentionally, they were preaching the
Word, just the Bible, symbolized by the fact that they regularly referred
to the Bible lying open in their hand.

In the vibrant mission church that Cragmor was, that's exactly what
Wayne Leys had done. That's what Al Negen meant when he knocked
me off my feet with his critical blast. Once I recovered enough to hear
him, I decided that I would experiment a bit with my preaching. I

began to preach with an open Bible in my hand, moving through the text verse-by-verse, pointing to this word and that, flipping pages from Genesis to Revelation, preaching the Word. Now that sermon on Ephesians 1:3–6 was not a theological discourse, but a careful examination of each word and phrase: "He chose us...He *chose* us...He chose *us.*" I would encourage people to turn in their Bibles to other places where the word *chose* occurred. A sermon on the fourth request of the Lord's Prayer in Matthew 6:11 would proceed slowly through each word: "Give...us...today...our daily...bread."

In this way, the congregation actually encountered the text, not just what I thought about the text. They studied the words of the Word, rather than merely listening to what I thought the Word meant theologically. A favorite verse for this style of preaching was Acts 17:11: "Now the Bereans were of more noble character than the Thessalonians, for they received the message with great eagerness and examined the Scripture every day to see if what Paul said was true."

It was a whole new way to preach. At first, I did it to be popular. I admit it. I was young; I needed their approval. The cocky young preacher who emerged from Calvin Seminary ready to change the world was being humbled. So I did what the congregation wanted, as interpreted by my partner in ministry. But as I did that, I learned a lesson about preaching that I've always remembered and tried to practice. Even after I stopped holding the Bible in my hand throughout the sermon (someone gave me a new Bible that was too big and heavy to make that practical), and even after I stopped moving slavishly word-by-word and verse-by-verse (later churches were put off by this preaching style, calling it a "Sunday School" approach), I continued to emphasize what the Bible actually said.

I became convinced that it is not enough, even in a highly educated, biblically literate congregation, to preach the truth. The preacher must demonstrate that the truth comes from the Bible. I've heard many powerful sermons over the years that were clearly true, but not clearly biblical. They were more a demonstration of the preacher's theological acumen, cultural savvy, and verbal eloquence than of the Bible's clear teaching. Especially now in this postmodern age, where truth is relative and personal, the audience must be able to see how the truth being preached comes not from the preacher's brilliant mind, but from the Bible's actual words. If they don't, they will begin to question the truth itself. After all, why should the opinion of the preacher matter more than anyone else's?

Preachers come and go, societies change, new emphases ripple through the church, children are born into congregations, new converts join. The one constant is the Bible. So Paul's words to his first-century protege in Ephesus are important for preachers of every age and place: "Preach the Word." In this second big turn on the mountain road to good preaching, I learned that I have to make sure the people read the text of the day, wrestle with it, understand it, and apply it to their own lives. Whether I actually hold the Bible in my hand or simply leave it open on the pulpit, I want to ensure they know that God's Word is the body and heart and soul of each sermon. Theology matters, of course. Knowing biblical and systematic theology will help you find the deeper meaning of your text and save you from idiosyncratic interpretations and applications of it. I never stop thinking theologically. But in Colorado Springs I learned to make sure that the Bible is central in the explication and application of the truth.

Al soon left his position as Director of Youth and Education to take over a ranch for troubled teens out on the high plains of Eastern Colorado. I've always wondered if it was because of me—because I wasn't Wayne, and Al just couldn't get over his deep admiration for Wayne. He said that wasn't it, and we did become good friends. Maybe he just needed to be even more of a cowboy. Anyway, Al left, but I'll never forget the way he forced me to turn a harrowing corner in the foothills of the Rockies and discover an exciting part of the landscape of preaching.

Now I knew how to preach the Word—I thought.

Chapter Four

TEACH

"All Scripture is God breathed and is useful for teaching."

II TIMOTHY 3:16

Al Negen taught me to teach the Word, or so I thought. Larry Jordan didn't agree. He and his lovely wife, Nancy, had recently been transferred by his company to Colorado Springs from Wisconsin, where they had been lifelong members and longtime leaders in the CRC. They quickly put down roots in the Springs and in Cragmor, Nancy playing the organ, Larry serving on the council. Attending both services every Sunday with both of their sons, they were an important working part of the team in that thriving mission church. They were warmly hospitable to my wife and me, so I saw them as allies and friends.

That's why I was so surprised one Sunday night after the service when they had been at Cragmor about a year. Nearly everyone had gone home, so it was just the three of us chatting at the entrance of the sanctuary. I don't recall what we were talking about, but I'll never forget Larry's words: "Stan, stop arguing with us. We already agree with the gospel. Teach us something so we can grow in our faith."

I was stunned by the suddenness and fierceness of his "attack." I felt betrayed by people I thought were supporters, a bit like David in Psalm 55:12–14: "If an enemy were insulting me, I could endure it; if a foe were raising himself against me, I could hide from him. But it is you, my close friend, with whom I once enjoyed sweet fellowship as we walked with the throng at the house of God." I was hurt, confused, and angry, which you will recognize by now as my standard response to such sharp correction.

Once my wounded ego had healed enough for me to drop my defensiveness, I began to think about what Larry had said. He had forced me to turn another corner on my journey, showing me that it's not enough to speak the truth in a theologically correct way or to preach the Word in a way that makes the Bible central to a sermon. Now there was this issue of *how* to do those two things: was I arguing or teaching, trying to prove that the Christian faith was true or simply teaching that faith in all its richness? I had assumed I had to do the former; Larry suggested there was another way.

Remember that I was in an extremely mission-minded church. Every Sunday I looked out at a congregation in which I knew there were any number of non-Christians. Our members were fantastic about bring their unchurched neighbors and fellow workers to church. We attracted dozens of new folks with repeats of that gargantuan VBS described earlier. We went into our neighborhoods, calling on people door-to-door using the Evangelism Explosion method of sharing the gospel. We asked those two famous questions developed by Dr. D. James Kennedy of Coral Ridge Presbyterian Church: "Have you come to a point in your spiritual life where you know for sure that you would go to heaven if you died? If you died and appeared before God and he asked, 'Why should I let you into my heaven?', what would you say?" Then we explained the gospel in a five-part presentation and called for a commitment to Christ. More than a few people responded positively.

Because of all this, there were presumably a number of nonbelievers in the congregation every Sunday, not to mention the new members who had just come to faith or the young people of the church who hadn't yet professed their faith. As a missionary pastor, I saw evangelism as my first calling, so all of my sermons were more or less evangelistic.

I explained that to Larry there at the door and intimated pretty directly that since he was from an old established CRC back in Wisconsin, he just didn't get it. He didn't understand the uniqueness of Cragmor. He didn't have a missionary heart. Just because he was convinced that the gospel was true didn't mean that everyone agreed. He needed to make allowances for the little lambs just finding their path and for the wandering sheep who had lost their way.

He graciously agreed with all that, but he continued to press his point. Besides the obvious fact that the old rams and ewes already in the fold still needed to be fed, Larry insisted that arguing was a less effective way of bring the lost into the fold than teaching. When you argue with people, trying to prove that they are wrong and you are right, they tend to get defensive. When you teach the Bible and its truth clearly and winsomely and relevantly, people can take it in, think about it, and make a decision without feeling badgered and backed into a corner. "If you teach all of us," Larry persisted, "the seeker and the unconvinced will be able to make a decision for Christ." He echoed II Timothy 3:16: "All Scripture is God-breathed and is useful for teaching."

I was not an easy convert to Larry's views on preaching. After all, Paul goes on in that verse to talk about "rebuking and correcting," and that can certainly be construed as arguing in some sense. Besides, apologetics was a favorite course in seminary; I loved all the deep and historical ways people had defended the faith and demonstrated its truthfulness to its cultured despisers. Doesn't the Bible urge us to "contend for the faith once for all entrusted to the saints" (Jude 3)? And finally, didn't Paul preach argumentatively, even in his first sermons? "Yet Saul grew more and more powerful and baffled the Jews living in Damascus by *proving* that Jesus was the Christ" (Acts 9:22, emphasis mine). Larry's problem, I continued to think, was his old-line CRC experience of the established church in which you don't have to press people for some kind of Damascus road decision for Christ, because eventually everyone will, like Timothy, come gradually to the faith through the patient modeling and teaching of grandparents, parents, and preachers (II Timothy 3:14–15).

What's the Difference?

Part of my problem with Larry's emphasis was that I couldn't quite envision how teaching sermons might differ from argumentative sermons. Thirty years later I can explain it pretty easily, but at the time I was confused. To help you wrestle with the issue, let me give you a few examples. In an early sermon on Genesis 1, I tried to prove that the theory of evolution simply could not be true because the text gives such a detailed description of God's creative work. I argued with the whole notion of evolution. In a recent sermon on the same text, while not in the least conceding the scientific battle to the atheistic evolutionists, I focused on the theological message taught by Genesis 1, rather than on the science.

Here's a sample from that second, teaching sermon. After reviewing a recent poll which reveals that the vast majority of Americans believe in some sort of divine creation but still want evolution taught in high schools, I sympathized with high school students: "For you, this is not merely an academic question. It is a very personal issue, because it touches on the central questions of your life—who am I, why am I here, how will I live my life?" The sermon focused on the way Genesis 1 answers those three questions: *who, why,* and *how.* Beginning with Genesis 1:1, I pointed out how often the first chapter of the Bible mentions God: "The story of creation is not first of all about *how,* but about *who.* The point is that it all came from God. That's what Genesis is about—*God* created.

"And *why.* Now you can talk about *why* in two very different ways. For example, there are two different ways to explain the boiling of water. You can say that it happens because of the rapid vibration of water molecules due to the application of heat. That's why water boils. Or you can say that it boils because someone wants a cup of tea. That's why water boils. The first speaks of physical process, the second of personal purpose. Genesis 1 and the rest of the Bible tell us why the world was created in that second sense—not so much the physical process as the personal purpose.

"And when the Bible *does* talk about the how, it simply says, 'He spoke.' Is that a clear and simple denial of the theory of evolution? The repeated emphasis on the Word of God in creation is not against science; it is against religion. Genesis was written to counter other religious explanations of the world—the religion of the Egyptians from whose clutches Israel had just been delivered, the religion of the Babylonians into whose clutches Israel would one day fall, the religion of the Greeks whose culture permeated the ancient world. Those religions taught that the world came into being because many gods fought or had sex or exerted themselves. Others said there were two equal forces in the universe from which all things came, while still others said that things have always been. As Israel walked through that religiously pluralistic world, God revealed the truth about creation in Genesis 1. 'In the beginning God, your God, Yahweh God created the world,' not by struggling, or fighting, or mating, or collaborating with other beings, but simply by speaking. This is not a scientific statement. It is a theological statement, a deeply religious statement. Indeed, as John 1 and Colossians 1 tell us, it is part of the gospel, for the world was created through 'the Word made flesh.'"

Although at this point in the sermon I am subtly arguing with atheistic evolution, I am doing so by teaching what the Bible says and means. The emphasis is on teaching.

Here's another example: in the mid-1970s my Easter sermon on I Corinthians 15 tried to prove that Jesus had risen from the dead. I spent all Easter morning trying to convince Christians that the Resurrection was historical fact. That, of course, is not a bad thing to do; indeed, given the annual attacks on the Resurrection in the Easter issues of major news magazines, it's a good thing to do. But a 2006 Easter sermon on Galatians 2:20 focused on teaching the congregation how the resurrection of Jesus impacts life today:

"On Easter Sunday two thousand years ago, we were resurrected from the dead, released from the cave, and deposited blinking in the sunlight, on a new street where a whole new life stretched before us. And our overwhelming reaction should be gratitude, deep exuberant gratitude for the power of the resurrection of Jesus that has changed everything for us."

Then I explained how Jesus has changed things in our lives, making some crucial distinctions introduced to me by a retired minister in my congregation who has frequently criticized my preaching (see chapter eight, "Gospel," for more about this helpful brother). He had read somewhere that the church has tended to focus on the birth and death of Jesus, on the cradle and the cross, while paying relatively less attention to the resurrection of Jesus, the gospel of the empty tomb. To be more specific, said my colleague, the church has stressed the reality of Jesus' resurrection from the dead (resurrection past) and the hope of our bodily resurrection (resurrection future), but not the effect of Jesus' resurrection on our lives day to day. And that is a serious thing.

Indeed, insisted my loyally opposed congregant, without that dimension of the Resurrection, the Good News isn't even good. "If you leave that out, then the gospel story only says: 'Jesus was born. Jesus died.' God said to man, 'There is the remedy. I fixed the problem. The slate is wiped clean. Now go and do a better job next time.' That's not good news. That is a tragic teaching."

In response to my friend's trenchant criticism, my new Easter sermon proceeded to teach what difference Jesus' resurrection makes for each day right now.

An early sermon on Ephesians 1:3–4 defended the uniquely Reformed understanding of election against Arminian attacks on that doctrine. The burden of the sermon was to prove that "our" doctrine was right. A more recent sermon on that subject focused on helping people appreciate the wondrous grace of God that has saved us from beginning to end. Rather than talking about "us" and "them," my aim was to help the congregation experience a sense of wonder at the amazing grace of God in loving us long before we loved him. I taught about the effectiveness of God's grace in the lives of spiritually dead sinners (Ephesians 2:1ff).

It took me a long time to be able to make such distinctions. The discussion about arguing versus teaching went on (in my mind at least) for many months, but Larry had certainly forced me to look at preaching from a different perspective. It's not enough to preach the Bible in a theologically intelligent way. You also have to think about *how* you are going to preach. Though I continued to think (and still do) that there is an important place for apologetic, even argumentative, preaching, two factors finally convinced me that it is more important, more often, to simply teach the Bible and its truth.

First, I was influenced by a most unlikely trio of preachers: Harry Emerson Fosdick, Robert Schuller, and Al Martin. Fosdick, of course, was that quintessentially modernist preacher from out east who, like most early twentieth-century liberals, denied the deity of Christ, the infallibility of Scripture, and other elements of the faith that I considered essential. But someone (I don't remember who, so I don't recall the motive) gave me a volume of Fosdick's sermons. I had heard that he saw preaching as pastoral counseling on a corporate scale. It was fascinating to see how his preaching aimed to make people psychologically healthy and whole. It was an entirely different way of preaching than I had ever heard.

Robert Schuller is the Reformed Church in America preacher who founded the Crystal Cathedral in southern California and is known all over the world through his expertly produced *Hour of Power* television program. While I was in Colorado Springs, I had the opportunity to attend Schuller's Institute for Successful Church Leadership in California. Sharon and I were part of a group of ministers and their wives who began the Institute very skeptical of Schuller because all we knew about him was his television persona. We all agreed that he had psychologized the gospel to the point where it was barely recognizable as the one we knew as Reformed Christians. The fullness of salvation in Christ had been transformed (distorted, we thought) into the power of possibility thinking.

But after five days with Dr. Schuller, we all had a deeper appreciation for what he was trying to do with his preaching. That's where he fits into this chapter. Like Fosdick, he helped me think about the *how* of preaching the gospel. How is it best done to reach the lost and help the found?

Al Martin would not want to be included in my unlikely trio of homiletical helpers. He was a powerful Reformed Baptist preacher in New Jersey to whom I was introduced by the Petersons back in St. Louis. They had given me a series of audio tapes I didn't pay much attention to at the time, but now the tapes came back to me. Martin was a throwback to the Puritan divines. A fervent and effective evangelistic preacher, he forcefully called people to conversion with a straightforward verse-by-verse exposition of biblical truth and a no-holds-barred appeal to come to Christ. It was a classically Reformed way of preaching to the lost in the tradition of Spurgeon and Jonathan Edwards. Here was yet another way of preaching that helped me think through the way I was going to preach after Larry's challenge.

Second, and more important, I began to study the preaching of the greatest missionary the world has ever seen, the missionary who introduced the entire western world to the gospel. I'm speaking, of course, about the Apostle Paul. Earlier I referred to the fact that the budding Paul "proved that Jesus is the Son of God" (Acts 9:22). Now I carefully studied his actual sermons in Acts to see how Paul proved the gospel and called people to believe in Jesus.

Paul clearly varied his method from audience to audience. For example, in Acts 17 he preached to the Jews in Thessalonica in a very different way than he did to the Greeks in Athens. To the Jews he made heavy use of the Hebrew Scriptures, while to the Greeks he made frequent references to their own religion and culture. But in spite of these different approaches to his diverse audiences, it became clear to me that Paul's preaching was always heavily didactic.

Though he did argue, even vehemently at times, his primary mode of preaching was to teach the facts of the gospel, using the Old Testament Scriptures when his audience was Jewish and the surrounding culture when they were pagan. In his teaching he might strive to show that his audience was wrong about something, but the burden of his preaching focused on who Jesus was and what he had done, what Jesus meant for the world, and what his audience should do about all that. He evangelized by teaching the Christian truth about Jesus. And, of course, Paul's letters, though they are full of correcting and rebuking, are first of all teaching. Most clearly in Romans, his magnum opus, and in Ephesians, his gem-like piece de resistance, Paul taught the indicative of the gospel before he pressed the imperative of the Christian life upon his readers.

So it happened that a businessman from Wisconsin helped me face a whole new issue. What is the most effective mode of preaching? Though, as I later learned, there are other questions about how best to teach, I learned at this bend in the road that teaching needs to be at the heart of preaching. So I would preach for the next seven years, until I found myself in the dust bowl of Byron Center, Michigan.

Chapter Five

WHY?

"What earthly difference does all this make?"

SHARON MAST

Before I tell you about the dust bowl I created for myself in Michigan and the critical comment that finally helped me dig my way out of the dust and get back on the road again, I must tell you about a dimension of preaching I've had to learn over and over again. I first caught a glimpse of this crucial aspect in St. Louis. I am reminded of its importance whenever I have great stuff with which to construct a sermon, but it simply will not come together. And I relearn it whenever I have preached what I thought would be a great sermon, but it just didn't seem to move anyone.

THE GREAT "SO WHAT?"

In those situations, the problem is almost always that I have not answered with sufficient clarity the great homiletical question, "Why?" Why do you want to say this to these people? It's not enough to know what you want to say or how you plan to say it. You must also be very clear on *why* you want to say it. You can have a carefully crafted arrow with a sharp point strung up in your bow, but if you don't know what you're aiming at, what your target is, what you hope to accomplish with that arrow, the great likelihood is that you'll hit nothing and nobody.

The first person to hit me with this question was my wife. She has always been my sharpest critic and my strongest supporter. That means she can say anything to me about my preaching, and has. However, like a tiger with her cub, she will rush to my defense if someone else is critical. I love her for both traits. Anyway, as I was wrestling with the truth issue back in St. Louis and producing sermons that were increasingly well-crafted theological dissertations, Sharon patiently listened as she played the organ in our little church or wrestled with our three-year-old and one-year-old in the pew. But as the weeks turned to months, her supportive smile turned increasingly tense, until it began to resemble a grimace. Finally, she could endure it no longer and quietly asked, "What earthly difference does all this make? You're telling us all this stuff, and it's obviously the truth. But what difference does it make for our lives?"

I'd like to tell you that my wife's impatient question shocked me into a new way of preaching, but it didn't, not at first. She wasn't a preacher, after all, or a theologian. I was. I was trained. And I had to answer to the "truth people" in my congregation. My wife was trained as a teacher, and I hadn't yet learned that teachers have a great deal to teach preachers. So while I heard her and acknowledged that there was some validity to her questions, I really didn't change the way I preached until Rev. Wilbert Van Dyk said basically the same thing.

While I was a student at Calvin Seminary, I had the privilege of working as a part-time intern under Bill Van Dyk at the Plymouth Heights CRC in Grand Rapids, one of the largest churches in our denomination at the time. Rev. Van Dyk already had a sterling reputation as a teacher and preacher of the Bible; I considered him the prince of preachers in the CRC. His sermons were masterpieces of biblical exposition, delivered with impeccable eloquence using nary a note, and always related in some practical way to the lives of his parishioners. I had the privilege of listening to him for two years, during which he made such a deep impression on me that people said for years afterward that I bore a vague resemblance to Bill Van Dyk—not physically, but as a preacher. I still consider that the highest compliment, even though I made no conscious effort to imitate him. Bill became my life-long mentor and friend. I'm delighted that things have come full circle, and my mentor is now a member of my congregation.

During my first years of ministry, while I was serving far away from all the resources of my seminary and denominational headquarters in Grand Rapids, I often called Bill for advice when I was facing some new and difficult problem. Somewhere in those early years, Bill and I were talking about preaching, and he introduced me to his version of Sharon's question. He called it the great "So what?"

"Before I finish preparing my sermon," he said, "I always ask, 'So what?' After I've said all this, what practical difference will it make in the lives of my people?" It was, of course, Sharon's question, but now that a great preacher and theologian had said it, I was convinced it was essential to great preaching. (And I have learned to listen to my wife in the first place. Though she's no professional theologian, she is a great student of human nature with an intuitive grasp of people and their relationships. And her visceral responses to gospel theology are a great corrective to my intellectual predilections.)

Plato and the Preacher's Perspective

I've since learned that there are two ways of asking this *why* question— from the perspective of the preacher and from the perspective of the congregation. First, why am I saying this? Yes, of course, I'm saying it because it's true and because it's biblical. But there are many facets of the truth and many texts in the Bible. So why have I picked *this* text, and why am I emphasizing this part of the truth?

If I don't know the answer to those questions, if I'm preaching on a subject simply because it is the lectionary lesson for this Sunday or because it is the Heidelberg Catechism Lord's Day assigned for that day, or worst of all, if I'm preaching on a subject just because I have to preach on *something* this Sunday, my sermon might be true, but it will surely be flat, dull, and perhaps even dead.

For as long as people have thought about rhetoric, we have known that speakers have different motives when they address others. Four hundred years before Christ, Plato identified three of these—to inform, to change, and to entertain. A lecturer in a university classroom might do the first, a salesman or military leader specializes in the second, and a comedian or after-dinner speaker often does the third. I come from a strongly theological, confessional tradition. In fact, the Church Order of the CRC requires that once a Sunday the preacher use the Heidelberg Catechism as an authoritative guide into the Scripture. This sixteenth-century Reformed confession is divided into fifty-two Lord's Days so that over the course of a year, the congregation hears the whole of the gospel. Understanding the truth is all important in this tradition.

Having used that catechism my entire ministry, I suppose it's not surprising that I preach many of my sermons to inform. In fact, if I don't intentionally think about it, that is almost my default motive. I want people to know the truth, because the truth saves. I want people to know the Bible, because the Bible is profitable for teaching, for correction and rebuke, and for training in righteousness (II Timothy 3:16–17).

Of course, that same text teaches that simply informing people isn't enough. There should be times when I want to correct and rebuke, and others when I want to train. In other words, sermons ought to aim at motivating people to change, not merely at passing on information to them. As Eugene Petersen says in *Eat This Book,* his typically refreshing explanation of *lectio divina,* "We are not interested in knowing more but in becoming more."[3] For far too many years, my sermons aimed at merely informing. I considered a sermon successful if I had clearly stated the truth so that people "got it."

Now, truth is the bedrock of the saving faith that changes lives. "You shall know the truth, and the truth will set you free," said Jesus in John 8:32. The strength of my theological tradition is this focus on knowing the truth. The second question and answer of the Heidelberg Catechism sets the tone for the warmest and most personal of all Reformed confessions: "What must you know to live and die in the joy of this comfort [of knowing Jesus Christ]? Three things: How great my sins and misery are; how I am delivered from my sin and misery by

Jesus Christ; and how I am to thank God for such deliverance." No wonder most of my sermons were focused on helping people know these three things. Such knowledge is crucial to the central comfort of belonging to Jesus.

However, just as there is more to preaching than passing on knowledge, so there is more to being a Christian than having a mind full of truth. Truth in our minds *ought* to make a difference, but it often doesn't. So the preacher must draw the connecting lines between knowledge and life, showing what difference a particular truth should make. Or to be Platonic, the preacher should actually aim to change people—not just fill their minds, but change something specific in their lives. After all, when Jesus preached "the kingdom of heaven is near," his first word was always, "Repent" (Matthew 4:17). Jonathan Edwards, the great eighteenth-century preacher, understood this motivational goal of preaching very well. He always insisted that preaching is the instrument by which God moves the human heart. That's why we preach the Scripture instead of just reading it.

Sermons might have quite different motivational goals. One sermon might aim at repentance, at actually moving the hearts of listeners to a deep sorrow for sin that will result in sincere resolution to change that sinful behavior. Another sermon intends to move the intellectual faith of the congregation that longest twelve inches in the world, from their heads to their hearts, so that they trust the Christ they know about. Yet another sermon aims to replace hate and hurt with love and forgiveness, another to change despair into hope, or sorrow into joy, or anxiety into peace. Sometimes a sermon aims to change the listeners' lives, rather than simply fill their minds.

Coming back to Plato's formula, there may even be times when the preacher is motivated to entertain the congregation. This motivation would have sounded far too worldly in the somber atmosphere of the strict Dutch Calvinism of my youth. However, I'm not talking here about trying to make people laugh (though in a grim world that doesn't seem like such a bad thing, does it?). Rather, I'm talking about trying to fill the congregation with delight, wonder, and joy at the goodness of the

Good News. Here the preacher isn't out to inform or motivate, but simply to help people enjoy God and celebrate his grace to us.

A sermon with this aim would be successful if the congregation could leave the service simply feeling positive, having taken delight in God, having tasted and seen that God is good. Granted, not every sermon can be motivated by such a goal. We are still about the truth, after all, and lives of faithful obedience. But there is surely a place for an appeal not to the mind or to the will, but simply to the emotions, to our sense of delight, to our appreciation for beauty. A balanced preacher will check his or her sermons on a regular basis to ensure that they aim at all aspects of human life—mind, will, and emotions.

The People's Perspective

This brings me to the second way of answering the *why* question—not "What is my motive?" but "What do I want to see happen in my listeners?" Asking *why* with reference to your audience will help you be more specific in your answer, more pointed in your sermon, and more powerful in your impact. If my motive is to inform, I must ask exactly what I want to happen in the minds of my listeners. Do I want to remind them of something they already know so their convictions are strengthened? Do I want to correct an error in their thinking so their doctrinal understanding is changed? Do I want to stretch their understanding of agreed-upon truth so their Christian mind is broadened? Do I want to alert them to deep but subtle challenges to the gospel in our society so they can be vigilant defenders of the truth? What difference am I trying to make in their minds?

Or if I want to motivate them to change, what change am I trying to effect? Do I want them to trust God more? Do I want to assure doubters that God will not reject them for their doubt? If I preach on the seventh commandment, am I urging adulterers to stop their sin, married couples to be more intimate, young people to be more cautious, or children to treat the opposite sex with respect and gentleness? At whom and at what am I aiming? Do I want to see discouraged people become more hopeful, wounded couples more forgiving, passive folks more passionate about justice, overwhelmed people more peaceful? You get the point. Knowing what I hope God will do in these beloved people through my sermon will not only shape and sharpen the sermon, but it will also fill me with a sense of passionate purpose when I open my mouth to speak the truth about Jesus Christ.

Of course, what the preacher intends and what the listeners come away with can be very different things. Quite apart from the distorting effects of sin, there is an incredibly complex communication grid through which all preaching inevitably passes. There is, first of all, what goes on in my head as I try to come to clarity about my own thoughts. Then there's the gap between my head and my mouth as I struggle to find the right words. As soon as my words leave my mouth, there is disturbance in the atmosphere into which my words fly—a passing fire engine, an adorably active two-year-old making faces at six pews of listeners, a sound system feeding back. And once the words actually reach the listeners' ears, there is a whole set of obstacles in their perception, understanding, and application of those words. Even if the listener actually hears exactly what I've said, there's still the issue of what he or she *thinks* about what I've said.

It's no wonder that weird things happen between the preacher's mouth and the listener's ear. That's why I thank God for the mysterious work of the Holy Spirit in the work of preaching. Constantly performing the miracle of homiletical transubstantiation, the Spirit transforms my ordinary words into something divinely inspiring, often with a very different result than I had so carefully planned. That is the joy and mystery of preaching. But that doesn't absolve me of the responsibility for doing my best. Over the years, I've learned that as I mount the pulpit, I had better have some clear idea of what difference I want to make in my people through this sermon, or else my preaching will lack power, commitment, and love. If I don't know why I'm saying this to them, why on earth should they listen?

I thank my wife and Bill Van Dyk for impressing this question on me. I wish I had learned their lesson infallibly. But I haven't. To this day, I get so wrapped up in exegeting the truth of the Scripture, organizing it into some form that I think will make sense, decorating it with enough pleasing things to make it attractive to bored listeners, and getting that sermon from my head to my heart that I forget to ask *why*? Whenever a good sermon goes mysteriously awry, the chances are that I forgot to ask this question. Whenever I forget the great "So what?", the sermon might be true and biblical and clear and even beautiful, but it won't make much difference in the lives of my congregation.

Knowing that as well as I do, you'd think I would have become a really good preacher by the time I left Colorado Springs. In those first six and a half years of my ministry I turned corners on my journey that showed me new vistas of *what, how,* and *why*. Thus, with a mixture of regret and gratitude, fear and excitement, I left the foothills of the Rockies to go to a place I did not know and did not want to be—Byron Center, the Garden Bowl of Michigan. Earlier, I called Byron Center a dust bowl, not because that's what it was in itself, but because that's what it became for me. You see, I had yet another corner to turn there on my journey to becoming a good preacher someday.

Chapter Six

ANGLE

"Tell it slant."

EMILY DICKINSON

The decision to move to Byron Center was one of the toughest of my life. I loved it in Colorado Springs. The sun shone three hundred plus days a year, the scenery was breathtaking, the mountains were a short drive away, and best of all for this young preacher, the church was exciting. Not only was it a happy flock of little lambs and old rams who loved each other, but it was also an ever-changing flock as dozens of wandering sheep found a home at Cragmor after being converted or revitalized in their faith. I really didn't want to go to West Michigan. In fact, I had driven through the little country town of Byron Center, surrounded by luxuriant vegetable farms, just six months before as we visited my wife's relatives. As we left, I said, "I'll never serve in a place like this." (I've since learned not to tell God quite so directly what I will and won't do.)

Having served out on the wild and wooly frontier of mission churches, I arrogantly and ignorantly assumed that there was no spiritual life in the staid established churches of the CRC in West Michigan. Now I had a call to a relatively new church on the outskirts of that little backwater village being rapidly transformed into a bedroom community of Grand Rapids. And I had to admit that I liked the people of Heritage CRC when I flew out for a pre-decision meeting with the congregation. I was caught between two "goods," and I absolutely did not know what to do. I weighed all the options, made long lists of pros and cons, talked to Sharon and friends, and of course prayed for guidance. Finally, in desperation I spent a day up in the Rocky Mountains in a cabin owned by the Navigators, a number of whom attended Cragmor CRC. There I had the longest sustained time of silence, study, prayer, and listening I had ever enjoyed in my life.

There, on a snow-covered mountain in a log cabin warmed by a blazing fire in a fieldstone fireplace, I heard God speak to me for the second time in my life. I can't tell you whether God speaks in a basso profundo rumble or a countertenor, but in an unmistakable way God said, "My presence will go with you, and I will give you rest." At the time I didn't know those were God's words to Moses in Exodus 33:14 as he faced a time of crisis out in the wilderness with those rebellious Israelites. But I listened to God's voice and came down the mountain convinced that I was supposed to go to Byron Center, a place I'd said I'd never go.

I tell you all that because I want you to know that the Heritage CRC in Byron Center did not start out as a dust bowl. It began as a God-directed partnership in which God kept his mountain promise to me and my family. Byron Center is sometimes called the Garden Bowl because its rich black muck produces multiple crops of luscious vegetables of all varieties. And that's what Heritage was for me and my family at first: a garden bowl of growth. We quickly took root and grew and flourished. The people were warm and earthy, deeply pious and yet filled with good humor, and we quickly made solid friendships that have endured to this day.

Best of all for a chronically insecure minister, they loved my preaching, and the church grew by leaps and bounds. (Of course, that wasn't surprising to me; after all, I had learned all about preaching in my first two churches.) I had arrived in Byron Center as a good preacher, and their support and encouragement only made me better. So we went along together for six gloriously happy years, abounding in grace and growth.

DRIER AND DRIER

Little did I know that I was getting drier and drier as a preacher. The public applause was unbroken, so I just kept doing what I had learned to do. Then my sharpest critic made one little comment that began another turn on my journey.

"You know," said Sharon, "you are starting to say the same thing the same way over and over again."

You probably won't be surprised to learn that my first response to her was anger, and then dismissal. I told her that it was perfectly Pauline for me to repeat myself. After all, Paul had said to the Philippians, "I don't mind repeating what I have written in earlier letters, and I hope you don't mind hearing it again. Better safe than sorry" (Philippians 3:1, *The Message*). I'm embarrassed to report that I concluded my angry reply with a personal attack. The problem was Sharon. She had been listening to me and only me for twelve years now, and she had simply grown accustomed to all my good stuff. So I dismissed my strongest supporter when she dared to contradict the crowds. But I didn't forget her comment.

That's why I was ready to listen when Ben Hoogendoorn took me out to lunch a short time later. Ben was one of the many builders in largely blue-collar Heritage, a high school graduate who made his living with his muscles and his manual skills. He and his family had befriended our family, taking us water-skiing on numerous occasions. He and I had even entered into a prayer partnership, meeting every morning at 6:30 for a month to pray for each other. We had become very close, and that, I suppose, is why he cared enough about me to take me out to lunch and tell me the truth. Softly, but bluntly, he said, "You're getting dry. You're saying the same thing the same way over and over again. You're drier than dust."

I didn't argue with him. At the mouth of two witnesses, the truth was established. But what could I do to get refreshed and begin growing as a preacher again? As I thought and prayed about it, it hit me that I hadn't read a serious book in over a decade, not since I left seminary. Oh, I had read newspapers and magazines and the occasional novel, but I hadn't bowed my head over a difficult book for twelve years. I was too busy doing ministry and learning to preach. So I decided that I would pick up my formal education again by enrolling in the Master of Theology program at my alma mater, Calvin Seminary.

That's where I turned a corner to see a whole new dimension of preaching. The first class I took got my mind working in high gear again; I went from zero to sixty in one class session. "Contemporary Trends in Christological and Trinitarian Doctrine" was taught by my seminary classmate and friend, Dr. Cornelius Plantinga, who has since become the president of Calvin Theological Seminary. It was, very simply, the hardest class I had ever taken in my life—not only because my brain wasn't accustomed to thinking about pure theology, but also because Neal made us read large chunks of heavyweight theologians like Barth and Rahner and then write papers critiquing what we'd just read. It made my head hurt, and it stimulated me as nothing else had in a long time. I was thinking new thoughts again.

During that ThM program, I studied much more theology, but the class that completed the turn in my preaching was "The Apologetic Theology of C.S. Lewis," taught by the delightful Dr. Ted Minnema. He divided the course into two parts—the nonfiction didactic works of Lewis (such as *Mere Christianity* and *The Problem of Pain*) and the imaginative fictional works (like *The Chronicles of Narnia* and *Til We Have Faces*). The purpose of the course was to have us evaluate which kind of apologetic literature worked best. We all concluded that the imaginative material was more effective because it didn't hit the opponent of Christianity head-on with the truth. Rather, it did an end run around his defenses and came at him from an angle.

By being creative and charming and lively, Lewis's imaginative works helped people believe the gospel. I now see that Lewis was simply imitating his Master, who according to Mark 4, never taught without a parable. Jesus did teach in other ways, but a parable was always in the mix somewhere.

That was a revelation to me, as I had always eschewed such an approach. In fact, I had often introduced sermons in Byron Center by saying, "This sermon is not going to be interesting. It will be true and biblical and clear and relevant. If you're looking for interesting, you won't find it here."

Sometimes I said that simply because I didn't have anything creative or imaginative to add to the sermon. But most of the time I said that because I didn't think being interesting was necessary. Just preach the Word in the way I had learned to do it, and that ought to be good enough. In fact, going beyond that might pander to the very thing Paul had warned about in II Timothy 4:3: "The day is coming when men will not put up with sound doctrine. Instead, to suit their own desires, they will gather around them a great number of teachers to say what their itching ears want to hear."

Paul was one of the most effective preachers the world has ever heard and he said, "When I came to you, brothers, I did not come with eloquence or superior wisdom as I proclaimed to you the testimony about God…My message and my preaching were not with wise and persuasive words, but with a demonstration of the Spirit's power, so that your faith might not rest on men's wisdom, but on God's power" (I Corinthians 2:1, 4). That's how I had tried to preach—just the truth, the truth pure and simple, in the power of the Spirit.

TELLING THE TRUTH SLANT

Now it seemed that God was showing me something else: not that I should stop preaching the truth pure and simple while relying on the Holy Spirit, but that there is another way to preach purely and simply with the Holy Spirit's power. Instead of only coming right at people with clearly reasoned arguments, a preacher can approach the congregation from the side with creativity, appealing to the imaginative side of their minds. As I was thinking this through, Neal Plantinga said to me, "You need an angle when you preach, some new way into people's minds and hearts." And he reminded me of Emily Dickinson's little poem, "Tell all the truth, but tell it slant."

So I began to work hard at making my sermons interesting, by using stories, word pictures, wordplay, and unusual approaches to familiar ideas. For example, as I preached through the CRC's "Contemporary Testimony," a quasi-confessional twentieth-century update of the classic sixteenth- and seventeenth-century Reformed creeds, I explained the self-deceptive character of sin not by rational argument, but by briefly retelling C.S. Lewis's classic tale, *Til We Have Faces*. In the first part of the story, the speaker sees herself as the victim of everyone else's treachery, including the gods' (it's a retelling of a pagan Greek myth). In the second part of the story, she sees that she herself was the villain all along, "a great fat spider" sitting in the midst of everyone else's lives and devouring them. The congregation was spellbound—and convicted of their own arachnid qualities.

Making the familiar interesting is very hard work. I have found that the secret for me is nonstop reading—not just theology, but biography and poetry and novels and memoirs, anything that will open me up to different worlds, fresh ideas, new ways of saying familiar things. I've since attended a glorious seminar taught by Dr. Plantinga, entitled "Imaginative Reading for Creative Preaching," that encouraged wide reading and gave attendees the actual experience of linking such reading with lively preaching. For example, in a New Year's Day sermon on faith, I opened with that poignant line from the breathtaking introductory scene of *The Kite Runner:* "There is a way to be good again." After exploring the idea of "things not seen" from Hebrews 11:1, I ended with a children's book entitled *The Looking Glass* that powerfully illustrated the importance of faith as we approached a new year.

Other preachers may be able to keep themselves fresh by simply observing life very carefully. I've discovered that I'm not as good at that as I'd like to be, or as my wife is, which is another of many reasons God paired me with her. I have to keep reading, widely and deeply, or else I will say the same thing the same way again and again. And I will enter the dust bowl once more and become boring.

Apart from preaching heresy, there is no greater sin for a preacher than to be boring.

That's true because the Bible is manifestly *not* boring. The Bible is the most dramatic, creative, imaginative, dynamic book in the world.

God's revelation of himself in history in Jesus Christ is simply the greatest news, the best story, the world has ever heard. Recently, on a Bill
Moyers PBS special, atheist philosopher Colin McGinn was asked why,
if Christianity is false, two billion people believe it. McGinn replied, "It's
an awfully good story." Or as Emily Dickinson would say, the Bible is full
of slant. Think of Jesus' parables, for example, or the enacted parables
of the Old Testament prophets (Jeremiah buying the potter's house) or
the poetry of the Psalms (where hills skip like little lambs). Most important, the gospel itself is slant—God entering the world not head-on in
all his power, but as a helpless Jewish baby who would save the world
via a cross. To preach this fascinating book in a dry dusty way is a crime.
Our sermons have to be interesting if they are to be truly biblical.

For a while, as I was digesting this new perspective on preaching,
I argued with it. Why isn't it interesting enough to simply tell the story,
explain the fantastic truths, come at it head-on? Why do I need an
angle? Here's what I concluded: It would be enough to do what I had
always done if people were perfect. But they manifestly are not. The
Bible is perfect, intensely moving, and deeply converting, especially
when the power of the Spirit attends the preaching of the Word. But
people aren't perfect, and the preacher has to work hard just to get
people's attention, let alone their engagement and understanding, leading up to faith and obedience.

Think about it. Little children don't get it; they lack the life experience and cognitive ability and working vocabulary to understand the
Bible. Teenagers, because they are fully engaged in figuring out who
they are, often don't care about something so seemingly remote from
adolescent angst. Unbelievers are skeptical of the Book or ignorant of
its saving message. Young parents are preoccupied with their children.
Middle-aged folks are thinking about business, marriage, golf, retirement. Many adults already know the truth so well that familiarity has
bred boredom, if not contempt, with straightforward sermons. Some
senior citizens have become weary of preaching after hearing thousands of sermons, while others have become either hypervigilant or
overly broadminded about the truth.

Because the people to whom I preach the Bible are at so many different places, I need to make the sermon as lively as possible just to get their attention. How can I get them out of their own little worlds into what Eugene Petersen in *Eat This Book* calls the great, strange, wonderful world of the Bible in which God in Christ is at the center of everything? I've learned that it often takes an angled approach, something unexpected, fresh, "slant," so they can see the biblical world in all its beauty, vitality, and relevance. "Tell the truth, tell it slant." That's what I learned in my dust bowl.

Chapter Seven

NARRATIVE

"I love to tell the story."

A. CATHERINE HANKEY

As I finished my ThM at Calvin Seminary, I never dreamed that I would work there one day. But after nine years in Byron Center, I was offered the position of Coordinator of Field Education at Calvin. After fifteen years of pastoral ministry in three very different churches, developing in my preaching as critics and teachers helped me discover new vistas, I had the opportunity to help seminarians grow as I had. I jumped at it, even though it took me out of my own pulpit and turned me into a critic and teacher myself.

Being out of my own pulpit was very valuable, because it gave me the opportunity to step back from the urgency of creating two new sermons each week. Critiquing student sermons, listening to the sermons of many other preachers as my family searched for a home church, and guest preaching all over West Michigan gave me the opportunity to ponder again and again the mystery of preaching. Why do some sermons work while others simply don't? I knew what I had learned on my journey, but as I was faced weekly with the challenge of helping others learn, I realized how much I didn't know.

By now I knew I hadn't arrived as a preacher. For fifteen years, whenever I thought I had, I would turn a corner and discover a whole new dimension. As it is for so many preachers, the problem for me was

that I didn't know what I didn't know. As the extent of my ignorance
gradually dawned on me in those early days of my employment at
Calvin Seminary, I decided that I needed to go back to school to sit at
the feet of master preachers.

As I began to think about graduate schools with their PhD programs, I had a providential encounter with Rev. Duane Kelderman. A
highly regarded preacher at an historic church in Grand Rapids, Duane
had just finished a Doctor of Ministry program at Denver Seminary
with the nationally renowned preacher and homiletician, Dr. Haddon
Robinson. I had not even considered a DMin program, because at the
time they had the reputation for being a cheap and easy way to get a
"Doctor" in front of your name. But as Duane told me about the rigors
of the Denver program and the growth he had experienced in his own
preaching under Robinson's tutelage, I decided to pursue not the aca-
demically focused PhD, but the professionally oriented DMin. I am
now such a proponent of these programs that I encourage every
preacher who intends to remain a preacher to get a good, solid DMin
after five or ten years of active ministry.

My DMin at Denver Seminary helped me turn yet another corner
as it exposed me to the whole issue of sermon shape or organization. I
had never thought about that because I knew only one shape, the one
I had absorbed by osmosis as I sat in the pew Sunday after Sunday as
a young person. It was the same shape I had intentionally learned as a
seminarian in my preaching classes at CTS.

Though it is popularly and sometimes pejoratively known as "three
points and a poem," that old familiar shape is more properly called the
deductive method of preaching. After a very brief introduction
designed to gain the hearers' attention and interest, the preacher states
his theme for the sermon. For example, "Today I will explain how central the Trinity is to the Christian faith."

Then the preacher expands on that theme with a series of points,
ideally three to reflect the Trinitarian nature of the truth. These points
explain the theme by showing its component parts, illustrating it with
stories from Scripture or secular life, relating it to other dimensions of

the Christian faith, and applying it to the congregation's life. The conclusion usually summarizes the various points made and (hopefully) drives home the central point one last time, often with a poem. A deductive sermon on the Trinity based on the baptism of Jesus in Matthew's Gospel would not so much move with the flow of an exciting story as it would distill truths from the story: the Father sends, the Son comes, the Spirit empowers. Those truths would then be organized logically or theologically as points, rather than psychologically or according to the plotline of the story.

The deductive method is a time-honored way of preaching the Bible. It specializes in clarity and is thus an excellent way to teach doctrine and morality. It is sometimes not very exciting, and it is not necessarily the best way to motivate people or help them experience the reality of God. Deductive preaching is logical and thus satisfying to the straight-line thinker, but it doesn't appeal to more imaginative listeners because it lacks suspense and tension. This kind of preaching develops suspense only when it is done poorly, in which case the congregation is tense because neither they nor the preacher knows where the sermon is going. The only suspense in such sermons centers around the burning question, "When will this agony be over?" I'm sure that some of my sermons evoked that very question. But it was the only sermon shape I knew.

I had heard about its opposite, inductive preaching, in which the theme is developed bit by bit and revealed only at the end of the sermon. The congregation is led into the truth rather than being told the truth up front. I had even read Fred Craddock's seminal book on inductive preaching, titled simply *Preaching,* and had listened to him on tape or in person whenever I could. Though his way of preaching fascinated me, I simply couldn't do it myself, having been conditioned by twenty-two years of listening to deductive preaching followed by three years of formal training in that style at Calvin Seminary. Add in fifteen more years of weekly practice, and I was hopelessly stuck in that old method.

A NARRATIVE SHAPE

Denver Seminary provided the disciplined instruction and supervised practice I needed to learn another way to organize and shape sermons. At Denver I learned a species of inductive preaching called *narrative preaching*. After a couple of paradigm-shifting introductory courses that approached the church from a sociological rather than a theological direction, emphasizing the importance of understanding where the church is in the world so the preacher can help lead it where it ought to be, I began my advanced studies in preaching with Dr. Robinson. Continuing the emphasis on exegeting the church and the world as well as the Bible, Robinson inspired me with his passion, underlined the importance of having one Big Idea in each sermon, and challenged me to communicate more directly by throwing away my manuscript and speaking with no notes whatsoever. He is a master preacher, and he sharpened my skills considerably.

But the man who pushed me around the corner to a whole new way of preaching was Dr. Paul Borden, whose great passion was narrative preaching. I'm not talking now about using a lot of stories in a sermon, or preaching on a biblical story, or even making the sermon one long story. I'm talking about a whole new way of organizing a sermon. Borden taught me that I could shape a sermon not only according to the logical flow of ideas, but also according to the psychological flow of events. As a form of inductive preaching, the narrative sermon does not announce the Big Idea at the beginning. Rather it leads the listener to the Big Idea, not by logic, but by the dynamics of story.

Since learning this method of sermon shaping, I've taught a couple of courses at Calvin Seminary in narrative preaching. Students are always puzzled about the exact difference between narrative preaching and inductive preaching. I tell them that narrative preaching is a form of inductive preaching, a species of the genus called inductive preaching, but that not all inductive preaching is narrative in character. Inductive preaching connects pieces of evidence to reach a conclusion logically, so that A plus B plus C equals D (D being the Big Idea in the sermon). Inductive preaching doesn't necessarily focus on the dynamics of plot. It follows a logical progression of ideas rather than the psychological order of events in which suspense or conflict is the driving force, as is the case in narrative preaching.

Dr. Borden used Eugene Lowry's groundbreaking books, *The Homiletical Plot* and *How to Preach a Parable*, to show me how to use the five classic elements of a good story in a sermon. Lowry makes those five elements memorable by calling them the *Oops*, the *Ugh*, the *Aha*, the *Whee*, and the *Yeah*. In the *Oops*, the preacher begins by creating some sense of disequilibrium so that the listener is off balance and wondering what will happen next. In the *Ugh*, the problem introduced by the *Oops* is deepened, the conflict gets more complicated, the suspense tightens as things get worse and worse. Then comes the great reversal, the *Aha*, as the conflict is turned around by grace breaking in, as God acts. The *Whee* is the working out of God's grace, as salvation is revealed and realized in the lives of the characters so that we experience in the story the joy and delight of salvation. Finally, the *Yeah* is the satisfied settling-in as we see what life is like after salvation has occurred. The problem is solved, the conflict resolved, because God has acted and salvation has come. So we say, "Yeah! That's how life ought to be."

For example, back in 1993, I preached a sermon on John 21:1–19 entitled "The Friend of Sinners and the Fallen Leader." I opened with this *Oops:* "Long before Jim Bakker, Jimmy Swaggart, and the thousands of other Christians who have stained the pages of church history with their greasy failures, there was Simon Peter. From that first day when his brother Andrew invited him to come and see Jesus, he had been the leader among the disciples. Now he had led them in failure." The rest of the *Oops* detailed Peter's failures at the end of Jesus' life, concluding with, "He knew that he had to live the rest of his life with that stain on his conscience. Nothing could erase it. He couldn't even say he was sorry, because Jesus was dead and gone."

But then came the *Ugh*, in which the problem or tension in the story is deepened. "At least, that had been his frame of mind all that Friday and Saturday and into Sunday. But then came a report that filled him with a tornado of whirling emotions." Now Peter had to deal with a Risen Christ, and that presented a whole new problem. "What would Jesus say to him? Or would Jesus even want to see him after his colossal failure?" The sermon traced the various post-Resurrection encounters, in which Jesus said nothing directly to Peter but did utter that mysterious command: "Go tell the disciples and Peter that I will meet them in Galilee." It seemed that Jesus had not forgotten the terrible failure of his lead disciples, and ominously, he meant to deal with them in Galilee.

The *Aha* occurs on the shore of the Sea of Galilee, where Jesus had prepared an early breakfast for his fishing disciples. At first there was not a word to Peter, even though he clambered overboard and swam to see Jesus. And then the silence was broken by Jesus' famous question: "Simon, son of John, do you love me?" That's the *Aha* in the sermon, the place where grace breaks through the failures of this fallen leader, because the great question for him was not "What did you do?" or "What will you do?" but "Do you love me?" The grace that came to Peter did not demand performance or behavior. It did not fixate on the past or the future. Grace came offering a new relationship in spite of the failure.

The *Whee* of the sermon focused on how this new relationship would affect the rest of Peter's life, on how his life would be changed by grace. "Feed my sheep," said Jesus. My sermon continued, "And with that Peter is not only a fisher of men, but also a feeder and protector and leader of those who have been pulled out of the sea of sin and made into sheep. Even after such terrible failure, the Big Fisherman is restored to leadership in the company of the disciples. Amazing grace!" I concluded with the *Yeah,* in which we are assured of the long-term effect of such grace in our own lives. "Let us celebrate the amazing grace of the Friend of Sinners, whose resurrection makes possible the restoration of cowards, deniers, and others who have sinned so spectacularly that they are afraid of meeting the Savior."

I found this way of shaping a sermon to be exhilarating and exhausting. Narrative preaching excited me because it was so new to me, but also because it was so old. As I researched this subject for my doctoral dissertation, I discovered how central narrative is to the Bible. That reassured me, because I had been a bit suspicious of narrative preaching at first. The whole concept of narrative in the larger theological world was often an alternative to the kind of propositional theology with which I was raised. You don't claim to know propositional truth about God; you simply deal with the story where the truth happens. There was narrative theology, narrative ethics, narrative history, and, of course, narrative preaching—all of it a way to dodge the straight-on propositional revelation of my classic Calvinistic upbringing.

That's not what Denver Seminary was teaching. Borden was simply helping me get in touch with the narrative character of the Bible itself. In terms of genre, the Bible is more than half narrative, though the narrative is of different types—history, gospel, parable. More importantly, the Bible itself is a great story, a metanarrative shaped by the plot of Creation, Fall, Redemption, and Restoration, which are as close to Lowry's five exclamations as you can get. It was exhilarating to preach in the same way God had shaped so much of his Word and in the way he redeemed the world.

But it was also exhausting, because I had preached the old deductive way for so long, and my church had come to expect that kind of preaching. By the time I was ready to do my DMin project and write my dissertation, I had left Calvin Seminary to take a call to the LaGrave Avenue CRC, a 1100-member church in downtown Grand Rapids. A classic city-center church with a neo-Gothic cathedral look, LaGrave was planted in the heart of the downtown area way back in 1887 as a Reformed witness to the larger community. Surrounded now by crumbling structures from the old downtown and sparkling new buildings from the remarkable urban renewal of the last fifteen years, LaGrave ministers to both the poor, living in missions and single-room occupancy hotels, and the powerful, living in upscale lofts and condos in the reborn city, as well as to the middle-class folks living all over West Michigan. It provides what a friend called "high church liturgical worship in a street-level ministry setting." It is a very traditional church with a ministry that is in many ways progressive.

For my dissertation project, I preached ten narrative sermons in an effort to change that traditional CRC into an even more dynamic out-reaching church. Like most immigrant churches, the CRC was for much of its history concerned mostly (though not only) with its own internal affairs, with caring for "the flock." Thus, it had a pastoral self-image. The communication theory behind my project was that the best way to change such an historic self-image was not through head-on argument, but by doing an end run around defenses with great stories of outreach, preaching slant as C.S. Lewis did in his fictional works. So I preached six sermons based on the life of Jesus and four on the history of the early church in Acts. In each sermon I pointed out that Jesus and his early followers were "friends of sinners," because that was the new self-image I was trying to hang in the mental gallery of my church. It was very difficult, and it didn't work. Looking back, I realize it couldn't have. You don't change one hundred years of history and tradition or a lifelong self-image in ten weeks.

The most interesting and painful thing about the project, however, was the reaction—both of the congregation and of myself. While some of the young people absolutely loved it, most of the adults were either confused or filled with consternation. One high-powered insurance executive said, "What in the world are you doing? That was like a Sunday School lesson. What happened to your usual incisive analysis and careful explanation?" And a PhD in literature almost screamed in my face, "That wasn't biblical. It wasn't Reformed. It wasn't even *you.*"

I had to agree with the latter comment. It wasn't me. By that, I don't mean only that it wasn't my habitual way of preaching, learned in my youth and at Calvin Seminary. It also wasn't, and isn't, my natural voice, my native way of thinking and speaking. I am a straight-line thinker, logical, analytical, deductive. If left to myself, I work at straight-edged clarity of explanation, not rabbit-warrened intricacy of plot.

Though I love a good story (novels are my favorite reading), and though I use stories in sermons as often as I can find good ones, I'm not by nature a storyteller. I can preach narrative sermons, and sometimes

I do, but I'm more inclined to use the dynamics of plot within deductive or inductive sermons. That is, even when I'm not preaching on a story, I may use Lowry's five interjections to build suspense and resolution into a sermon that announces the Big Idea up front (deductive) or arrives at it only at the end (inductive). This kind of sermon won't sound like a story because it lacks scenes and characters and a plotline, but it will feel like a story because it uses the psychological dynamics of one.

Playing Your Own Instrument

Discovering this about myself was a side benefit of the Denver experience. I'm convinced that all of us have natural gifts we use without thinking and potential gifts we can develop through training and experience. The latter will never be natural to us, though we can learn to use them. For example, Dr. Robinson's insistence on "no note" preaching fits his natural gift for extemporaneous speaking, while my anxiety about misspeaking makes a manuscript a necessity if I'm going to communicate clearly and smoothly. I can speak without notes, but it's not natural to me, so I don't do it. The same thing is true of narrative preaching. I can do it, but it's not natural.

I've learned that you should use the gifts you've been given, play the instrument you're good at, be yourself. That doesn't mean that I should stick stubbornly to my habits. I must be open and able to stretch. Who knows but that some hidden gift will emerge that will make me a much more effective preacher. But there's nothing wrong with—and indeed, there's great comfort in—discovering your natural voice, your native way of thinking, your best God-given gifts, and then being yourself.

The main benefit of the Denver experience was learning that there are more ways to shape a sermon than I had ever imagined. For that matter, there are more ways to tell a story than slavishly following Lowry's five exclamations. Some postmodern stories, for example, seem to ignore plot entirely, preferring to follow the random meanderings of the mind or to paint a series of imagistic experiences that go nowhere and seem to mean nothing. But it was important to my growth as a preacher to be confronted with the thought that different genres of Scripture might require different shapes of sermons. Similarly, different learning styles and the theory of multiple intelligences have implications for using different sermon strategies.

The wonderful diversity of literature and life opens up all kinds of possibilities for sermon shape. For example, I have been greatly stimulated by Paul Scott Wilson's *The Four Pages of the Sermon*. It has provoked me to think deeply about another matter with which I shall deal in the next chapter: namely, what it means to preach the gospel. Wilson's book presents a delightfully simple but provocatively fruitful way of shaping sermons that is neither narrative nor deductive. His fresh approach makes me wonder what other new shapes a postmodern age will suggest to us. I guess I'll just have to stay on the road—in hopes that someday I'll be a good preacher.

Chapter Eight

GOSPEL

"Woe to me if I do not preach the Gospel!"

I CORINTHIANS 9:16

S ometimes a mountain highway turns very sharply, and new vistas come into view so suddenly that they evoke a gasp of wonder or horror. We Coloradans call them hairpin turns, because they resemble those old-fashioned bobby pins ladies used in the days before hairspray and gels and hair clips.

But other turns are more gradual: long, sweeping turns in which the new perspective comes into view a degree at a time. It's the kind of turn described in the classic country song I heard back in my youth: "Give me forty acres and I'll turn this rig around." This chapter is about that kind of turn, a turn so slow and gradual that it seems endless. In fact, I'm still making it. It's the turn that has confronted me again and again with the whole issue of what it means to preach the gospel. What exactly did Paul mean by the phrase "preach the gospel" when he wrote, "Woe to me if I do not preach the gospel"?

One of the best compliments I have ever received as a preacher was, "You preach the gospel." That sounds like a simple compliment, I know, but you have to understand who gave it. The Reverend Jacob Eppinga is a legend in my denomination and my immediate predecessor at the LaGrave Avenue CRC. Jake had been in the ministry for over sixty years, thirty-four of those filling the pulpit at LaGrave in his inimitable fashion. He retired at seventy and preached nearly every Sunday into his nineties, when he died of cancer.

Jake is known all over the CRC because of his regular column in *The Banner,* the official magazine of our denomination. The title of the column gives instant insight into the delightful narrative way in which he preached the gospel for over sixty years. It's called "Cabbages and Kings," a phrase from Lewis Carroll's *Through the Looking Glass.* The thing you have to know about this legend is that he is also a gentleman, a Christian gentleman. That has been very important to me as his successor, because until he died, for the nearly twenty years I have filled LaGrave's huge pulpit, Rev. Eppinga remained a member of this church and a frequent attender at services in which I preached. Some of you may belong to denominations in which the former preacher is not allowed to remain a member of his congregation upon retirement because the presence and influence of that beloved old giant would threaten the ministry of the little David who follows. Horror stories about former ministers ruining the ministry of their successors are legends throughout the Christian church. I personally know ministers whose tenures in a new church have been significantly shortened by the presence of the former pastor.

But that never happened with Jake, because he was a complete Christian gentleman. Even when he disagreed with me, he didn't tell a soul—including me! He was almost unfailingly quiet and unobtrusive, hiding his feelings behind a poker face that would be very valuable in these days of high-stakes poker on ESPN. So, several years ago when I asked Jake how he thought things were going at LaGrave under my leadership, I was deeply touched when he said positive things and concluded with his highest compliment: "You preach the gospel."

What Is the Gospel?

I wondered then exactly what he meant by that, and not for the first time. Over the years I have been confronted again and again by the deceptively simple questions: "What is this thing called the gospel? And what does it mean to preach that gospel?" So many books have been written about the former question that only a naïve preacher would claim the answer is obvious. However, as I have wrestled with it over the years, I have always come back to the words of my lifelong ministry mentor, Bill Van Dyk: "Every sermon should be about Jesus." Whether your text is Old or New Testament, wisdom literature or apocalyptic, prophecy or Gospel, history or epistle, the main point must always be Jesus. You haven't preached the gospel until you have preached about Jesus.

That simple guideline has served me well, but it has not gone unchallenged. In my days at Calvin Seminary as Coordinator of Field Education, many a lunch conversation at the faculty table was occupied with this very question. One of the Old Testament professors in particular was adamant in his opposition to the simplicity of "preaching Jesus."

"Preach the text!" he would virtually shout. "Preach the unique text that is in front of you. If you press every text into the preconceived mold of that simple formula, you will not preach the whole Word of God to your people. Study that particular text. Hear what it said to the original audience. And preach that narrow slice of the truth of God to your congregation today. Don't force Jesus into a text where he isn't found. Preach the Word of God that is in that text."

I learned much from his challenge. It is absolutely true that a simplistic focus on "Christ and him crucified" can blind us to the many-splendored wonders of the whole counsel of God. After all, when Paul said to the Corinthians that he had resolved to know nothing among them "except Christ and him crucified," he went on to say that he did "speak a message of wisdom among the mature" (I Corinthians 2:4–6) The stern proclamations of my Old Testament friend (who bears a striking resemblance to what I imagine Elijah looked like) reminded me that the gospel is about a lot more than the cross of Christ.

Yet I remain convinced that Jesus must be in every sermon, because he himself said that he is in every text, if only we have the eyes to see him. When he was attacked by those experts in the Old Testament who could not believe that someone like him could be the Christ, Jesus explained the heart of the Old Testament: "You diligently study the Scriptures because you think that by them you possess eternal life. These are the Scriptures that testify about me, yet you refuse to come to me to have life" (John 5:39–40). I can't find Jesus in every single text easily or quickly. I think of purity codes in Leviticus or tales of terror in Judges or odd bits of wisdom in Proverbs. But I have found that if I can see that text in the light of the "Scriptures that testify about me," I can usually find a way to show how Jesus is at center of the Word of God to us in that text. If I don't, what I say may be true, but I won't be preaching the Gospel Truth.

Perhaps an example will help. In a recent series on the minor prophet Habakkuk, the second sermon was an exposition of Habakkuk 1:5–11, in which God responds to the prophet's anguished questions flung in the face of God. There seems to be no justice in the lives of God's people, because they are hemmed in by the wicked Babylonians. So Habakkuk cries, "How long, O Lord, must I call for help, but you do not listen? Why do you make me look at injustice?"

God answers Habakkuk by explaining that the invasion of the Babylonians is, in fact, God's doing. "I am raising up the Babylonians." I picked up on that picture and talked about God raising up a big ugly stick over his rebellious, disobedient child, entitling the sermon, "God's Big Ugly Stick." My point was that God often uses unexpected instruments to correct and save his people.

Here's how I concluded the sermon so that it was finally about Jesus. "The most magnificent example of the use of a big ugly stick to save the people of God is, of course, the cross of Christ. In fact, you would be surprised to know that in Acts 13:41, the Apostle Paul quotes Habakkuk 1:5 as a prophecy of what God would do in Christ. Think about it. God's way of saving us was as unexpected, as shocking, as unreasonable as anything God ever did in the day of Habakkuk. I mean, really! God became a man? Ridiculous! Saved by a criminal dying on a cross? Preposterous! And all you have to do to be saved is believe? How foolish! And yet that was God's way of saving us, by raising up a big ugly stick and nailing his Son to it. When you want to ask 'Why?' and 'How long?', behold the man on that big ugly stick."

It isn't always so easy to find Jesus in an obscure place like a minor prophet, because the New Testament doesn't directly refer to every single Old Testament passage. But I am usually able to preach Jesus if I remember Jesus' claim in John 5:39 that "the Scriptures testify about me," even if I have to spend the majority of my sermon time and effort on explaining that difficult text and its original meaning. Most of the sermon, then, isn't about Jesus, but in the end Jesus is the point of the sermon. That has worked for me for many years—but recently my way of blending the original meaning with the ultimate meaning has been strongly challenged.

How Much Jesus?

One of the challenges has come from a retired minister in my congregation. LaGrave is a treasure trove of retired ministers. With nearly two dozen of them, I have access to literally centuries of accumulated wit and wisdom, grace and truth. Nearly all of them are the most supportive and encouraging congregants any preacher could ever desire. They remember how hard it is to come up with sermons that satisfy all the demands of professional homileticians and all the needs of ordinary people, so they usually give me a hearty handshake, a warm smile, and a gracefully worded "Attaboy!" But not always, and not all of them.

One of them in particular has challenged me over and over on the way I preach Christ. "It's not enough to plug Jesus into the end of a sermon," he would say, referring to sermons like the one on Habakkuk. "That isn't preaching Christ. We don't get any sense of the glory, the magnificence, the fullness of redemption in Christ with that kind of preaching."

Even more than the question of how much Christ has to be mentioned before a sermon is gospel, this brother has asked, "Which part of Christ and his work is central to the gospel and to gospel preaching?" My immediate answer has always been "Christ crucified," because of the above quoted passage from I Corinthians 2. But my clergy critic vehemently insists that I have truncated the gospel. "It's the resurrection of Christ and the affect of that resurrection on life today that is central to the New Testament. You have to preach the Risen Christ and the work of his Spirit in raising the people of God to new life each day. Otherwise you haven't preached the gospel."

In spite of my defensiveness in the face of his continued efforts to correct me, I must confess that my friend has raised a very important issue with which I continue to struggle. I do not disagree with his insistence on the centrality of the Resurrection and the importance of the ongoing work of Christ's Spirit in our lives. Who could disagree? But I can think of other central themes in the gospel. The preaching of Jesus himself centered on the kingdom. "Jesus went into Galilee, proclaiming the good news of God. 'The time has come,' he said. 'The kingdom of God is near. Repent and believe the good news!'" (Mark 1:14–15). My Reformed tradition has emphasized that theme of the kingdom with a special focus on the sovereignty of God. Justification by faith alone was the major theme of the entire Protestant Reformation. And N.T. Wright, in his little chestnut of a book, *What Saint Paul Really Said,* insists that the gospel is not about what we must do to be saved, but about what God has done to save us, which cannot be summarized simply or briefly.

So I struggle with the question of what exactly the gospel is that I'm to preach. It's a big question, especially in this postmodern age when so many have no understanding of any of these key biblical themes. What truths are really central to gospel preaching? And how do we preach those central truths to an age that acknowledges no absolute truth? It is an absolutely important question, and I'm grateful to my loyal critic (though I'm not always happy with him) for raising this crucial question. He has studied long and hard on the road to his rock-solid convictions. That's something more of us preachers need to do as we continue our journey on this long and narrow highway that leads to good preaching. "Woe to me if I do not preach the gospel!" But what is this gospel that I must preach?

HOW TO PREACH GRACE

Another challenge to the way I preach the gospel has come through a book I've mentioned previously, *The Four Pages of the Sermon,* by Paul Scott Wilson. As I said before, it offers a fascinating way of organizing sermons. Each sermon should have four pages, says Wilson. Of course, he doesn't mean that a sermon must be exactly four pages long, but that every sermon should have four parts. At the risk of oversimplifying a richly detailed book, here's what he means: Page One deals with the trouble or problem (the sin or suffering) in the text. Page Two connects that textual trouble to the trouble in life today. Page Three shifts to God's grace in the text. Where do we see God active in this text in a saving way? Page Four focuses on God's grace in our lives. How is God active in that same saving way today?

I recently preached on Isaiah 55:12, "You will go out in joy," using the Four Pages schema. I explained that the trouble in the text is the exile of Israel. There was "no joy in Mudville," because God's ancient folk were huddled by the rivers of pagan Babylon. That was Page One. Page Two dealt with the ways in which we experience exile today, focusing on a very sad story of a man freed from prison after a DNA test proved his innocence, but who simply could not find joy in the outside world. We may be technically free, but we can't find joy because we are in exile from God. By paying careful attention to three rich images of deliverance scattered through Isaiah 55, Page Three explained how God acted to deliver his people from exile. Then I concluded with a focus on the way in which God leads us out in joy today through the work of Christ. That was Page Four.

The Four Pages approach is a most helpful way to organize both exegesis and exposition so that two things happen—the text is taken seriously and the congregation is addressed in the real situations of their lives. But this method has raised a large question for me about how to preach the gospel. Wilson insists that each sermon should end with grace, with the past, present, and future actions of God that save us. That makes sense to me, given the emphasis of my Reformed tradition on sovereign grace. As I've said before, God's grace in Jesus should be the point of every sermon. But does every sermon have to *end* with grace? That's the question. To preach Jesus in a biblical way, do I always have to end with an emphasis on grace? That troubles me for two reasons.

First, ending with grace clashes with everything I learned in my preaching classes. Though my professors may not have intended this, I learned that it is important to end sermons with application. After spending the majority of the sermon explaining the meaning of the text, you then apply that meaning to life in a practical way. This meant every sermon should end with something the listener should do—repent, believe, rejoice, love, be patient, read your Bible, pray, and most of all, accept Christ. Here's what you must *do* as a result of what this text says.

By contrast, Wilson seems to say that a genuine gospel sermon must end with the good news of what God has done, is doing, or will do. Directions for life come earlier in the sermon. You don't end a sermon with *oughts* and *shoulds,* with the duty of humans. That can easily lead to the bondage of works righteousness. Instead, you end with the deeds of God, the good news of God's actions. Something in me really resonates with Wilson, but his approach leaves me with an uneasiness. What about pressing the moral and spiritual claims of the gospel? If you always end with grace, what becomes of the practical implications of what God has done? I'm still struggling with my old training.

The second reason, much more important than my decades-old education, is the centuries-old wisdom of Paul, in whose letters Wilson's order is reversed. Paul spends the first half of his major letters to the Romans and Ephesians on grace and the second half on the implications of that grace for daily life. First "Here's what God has done for us in Christ," and then "Here's how we must live today." If Paul preached Jesus that way, isn't that how we should do it? Of course, one could argue that all of Paul's ethical exhortations were soaked in grace, so he really did emphasize grace. And that is certainly true. But the question that plagues me is precisely how do I preach that grace, how do I preach Jesus in a biblical way? What's the order? What's the emphasis?

Now, it may well be that I have oversimplified or misunderstood all the ramifications of Wilson's homiletics, and for that I apologize. I have not intended to provide a professional critique of his fine book. But his book has personally challenged me to think afresh about the whole matter of gospel. I really do feel as Paul did: "Woe to me if I do not preach the gospel!" But how do I preach the gospel so that God's saving grace in Christ is central in all its magnificent beauty *and* so that the life-changing implications of that salvation are pressed upon grace-saved sinners with all urgency? Jesus had the indicative and the imperative perfectly balanced. "The time has come. The kingdom of God is near. Repent and believe the good news." So as I continue on my winding, sometimes confusing road to good preaching, all I can do is pray for his guidance.

Chapter Nine

PASSION

*"The best lack all conviction, while the worst
are full of passionate intensity."*

W.B. YEATS

These words from Yeats' famous poem "The Second Coming" are part of his description of the world in the chaotic days following WWI, a world where things were falling apart and the center could not hold. It is a testament not only to his poetic genius, but also to his prophetic insight that those words still ring true nearly a century later. And they highlight a major discovery along my mountain road to good preaching. I learned it early, and I have relearned it many times since. Since I've alluded to it often in other chapters, I had not planned to spend an entire chapter on it. But then I had a peculiar dream, and in true biblical fashion, it seemed like a word from God encouraging me to focus on this part of preaching.

Like most dreams, this one was filled with a lot of images and events that didn't make much sense. I was in some sort of resort beside a river, surrounded by lots of folks I didn't know from Adam. I can't remember all the strange events that happened, just that they made me very tired and stressed. But I do vividly remember sitting on a bench beside a river when someone tapped me on the shoulder and said, "Listen as I tell this guy what has been wrong with your preaching the last two years." I turned around, and there was Rev. Jacob Eppinga, my predecessor at LaGrave, pointing to an unknown man.

I spoke of Rev. Eppinga in the last chapter. As I said then, he was the perfect Christian gentleman in his ongoing membership at the church he had led for thirty-four storied years. I'm not an interpreter of dreams, but I suspect that Jake was there in my dream because he was almost not there in my life. He had just discovered that he had a deadly form of cancer, and at the age of ninety-one, things didn't look good for him. In my nearly eighteen years at LaGrave, he had never uttered one negative word of criticism to me. But now, as he prepared to fall asleep in the Lord, he was in my sleep pronouncing a devastating critique of my recent preaching. Speaking toward that other man, but straight at my heart, he finished his dream speech with these words. "For the last two years, your preaching has been all about preparation, rather than prayer."

Ordinarily, I don't pay a lot of attention to my dreams; I'm not much of a mystic. But this was Jake speaking, after all. And what he said rang true, even though I hadn't really thought about it until that voice weighed me and found me wanting. I do pray, and often. When I preach, I pray before I begin to prepare, and I pray before I begin to preach what I've prepared. But as Rev. Eppinga said, I didn't pray nearly as much as I prepared. I was spending much more time studying the written Word of God than I was talking to the God who speaks in those pages.

This imbalance produced sermons that were biblically correct, theologically orthodox, culturally informed, personally relevant, verbally polished, and even interesting (at least, when I prepared well. I wish I could tell you that I *always* prepare well, but I'm trying to be honest in this book). But even the best of them were not always powerful, because they lacked passion. I knew better. I had learned the importance of passion in preaching over and over again. But apparently I hadn't learned it well enough, because God had to send a dream to remind me of something I had seen many times before on my journey.

PASSIONATE PREACHERS

Way back in St. Louis, my Reformed Baptist friends shared those immortal words of the Puritan preacher, Richard Baxter: "I speak as a dying man to dying men, as never to speak again." I was moved by those deeply passionate words about the task of preaching. They summed up the kind of passion I had seen in the Christ of the Gospels, whose sermon about the purpose of the temple was accompanied by overturned tables and fleeing moneychangers (Matthew 21:12–13), whose sermon about his own power over death was delivered in a voice trembling with rage at the invasion of death into the lives of those he loved (John 11:33–34), whose sermon to the hypocritical Pharisees was filled with thunderous "woes" (Matthew 23), whose sermon to the grieving women about the coming destruction of Jerusalem was undoubtedly delivered with a catch in his throat (Luke 23:27–31).

Over the years, I've heard our Lord's passion echoed in Paul's spoken and written sermons, as, for example, in his brave call to repentance in the midst of the intellectuals at Athens (Acts 17) or his frustrated question to the Galatians, "O foolish Galatians, who has bewitched you?" (Galatians 3:1). I hear his passion about the whole enterprise of preaching in his letters to the Corinthians and the Philippians:

"Yet when I preach the gospel, I am compelled to preach. Woe to me if I do not preach the gospel."
I CORINTHIANS 9:16

"Since, then, we know what it is to fear the Lord, we try to persuade men. For the love of Christ compels us."
II CORINTHIANS 5:11, 14

"It is true that some preach Christ out of envy and rivalry, but others out of good will. But what does it matter? The important thing is that in every way, whether from false motives or true, Christ is preached. And because of this I rejoice."
PHILIPPIANS 1:15–18

I'm always moved by Paul's stirring charge to his young protege and to every preacher since: "Preach the Word: be prepared in season and out of season, correct, rebuke, and encourage—with great patience and careful instruction" (II Timothy 4:2). I didn't need a dream to convince me of the importance of passion in preaching. But I did need reminding, because under the tyranny of the urgent requirement that I have two sermons ready every Sunday, I had forgotten the ultimate importance of Holy Spirit-produced passion. I had neglected those basic guidelines for gospel preaching laid down by Paul: "My message and my preaching were not with wise and persuasive words, but with a demonstration of the Spirit's power" (I Corinthians 2:4). I've repeated that turn on my mountain highway a number of times. I know, Jake, I know.

But even when I remember the importance of passion in preaching, I still struggle with a couple of key questions. What is this thing called passion? And where does one get it? I've discovered that passion is notoriously hard to define. I'm reminded of the judge who was asked to define pornography back in the early days of the struggle to stem the rising tide of that cesspool. When challenged by lawyers and reporters, he said, "It's hard to define, but I know it when I see it." It isn't easy to agree on what passion is either.

For example, several years ago, LaGrave joined with five other local churches in a joint effort to become intentional about spiritual growth. We used the Natural Church Development material written by Christian Schwartz, who has discovered that church growth comes not from this program or that strategy, but from certain "quality characteristics." In his research, he has found eight such quality characteristics that result in natural church growth. One of them is "passionate spirituality." Our six churches distributed questionnaires to a sizable segment of our leadership and sent off our completed forms to the NCD scorers. When they were returned, we were shocked to discover that the lowest score for every church was in passionate spirituality.

Now, these were six very different churches in terms of size, worship style, ministry location, leadership, corporate culture, and more. And yet according to these questionnaires, we all lacked passion. Perhaps we really did, but as we investigated further, we learned that the

NCD folks defined passionate spirituality in terms that almost guaranteed low scores for us at this point in our denominational development. For example, the NCD folks measured passion by how many people a church had in small groups. That may well be a good indicator, but our denomination has only recently caught on to small groups. Until the fairly recent past, our churches were so family oriented and had such a strong system of men's and women's societies that small groups weren't necessary. Does the lack of small groups in our churches mean that we aren't passionate in our spirituality—or just that we are way behind the learning curve? Not wanting to trust our interpretation of the questionnaires, however, we all resolved to preach a series of sermons on passionate spirituality to remedy our low scores. And guess what? Those sermons were wildly different, because all six of us defined passion very differently.

On another front, a fine, spiritually mature member of my church is always saying we need more passion in our worship. He came here from an inner-city church with an informal worship style that features gospel music, a great deal of call-and-response congregational involvement, and very emotional (and physical) preaching. Even though he joined us because he had finally wearied of that kind of worship, he still says to me frequently, "Where's the passion here?" But when I ask him what that means, he has a very hard time spelling it out. "I know it when I see it"—which doesn't help this preacher very much as I strive to be more passionate.

But I have to try, if for no other reason than to attract and keep young people. A couple of years ago, LaGrave received a grant from the Calvin Institute of Christian Worship to study how a church like ours, with formal liturgical worship, can involve teens in the life of the church and in lifelong Christian discipleship. We're deeply committed to our worship style and to our young people, so we wanted to discover what we could do to keep both. We read relevant books, talked to national experts, visited a number of churches, and interviewed our own teens. It was a very fruitful study for a variety of reasons, and a disturbing one for me as a preacher. We discovered a number of surprising things, the most disturbing of which was their emphasis on passion. "Teens are heat-seeking missiles," said Jane Rogers Vann, one of our consultants. "They will go where there is fire."

Again and again in our research, we heard that the most important thing in worship for teens is passion—not worship style (as conventional wisdom insists), but passion. Why would that disturb me? Because, according to our research, teens are looking for passion most of all "up front," in the leaders and particularly in the preacher. Much more important than musical selections or the use of technology or the age of the leaders was the passion of the preacher. And that heightened for me the importance of the question, what exactly *is* passion in preaching? Is it conveyed in the volume of the preacher? Is it an issue of emotional displays? If so, what emotions convey passion? Is it passion in gestures or body language or movement? How can I convey passion when I am a more-than-slightly balding sixty-three-year-old preacher who wears a clerical robe while standing in a massive pulpit that looms over the congregation, backed up by a choir singing classical music to the accompaniment of a 109-rank pipe organ in a neo-Gothic cathedral?

WHERE DOES PASSION COME FROM?

In an effort to make my definition of *passion* a bit less subjective (and defensive), I decided to check out the Greek word behind the word. It is the word *pathos,* which my Greek dictionary tells me has to do with experience, and particularly the experience of suffering. If preaching is to be passionate in that ancient biblical sense, then it must be rooted in experience, and particularly the experience of suffering. I will be passionate if I have experienced what the text is talking about, if I have felt the impact of the message on my own life, if the heart and soul of the message resonates with my own heart and soul, if I have thought and prayed deeply enough to allow the text to touch my emotions. I will be passionate if the Bible passage has made me suffer sorrow or anger or love or joy or peace.

Genuine biblical passion in preaching cannot be created, and it is not expressed primarily in a dramatic use of voice or body. It cannot be manufactured by atmosphere or technology. Even excellent performances by musicians and corresponding praise by the congregation cannot produce biblical passion. Passionate preaching comes from a deep experience of the gospel that has touched the heart and soul and emotions of the preacher.

That little word study helped me give some substance to this elusive thing called passion. As I've thought about it more, I've realized that whenever people are genuinely moved by a sermon I give, when their hearts are touched and their emotions are stirred and their lives are changed, two things are always true. First, I myself was first deeply convicted about that sermon, about the truth of it and the importance of it, about what I wanted to say and why I wanted to say it. Passion grows out of heartfelt conviction about Jesus, the Bible, and this particular text. Of course, every preacher should always be convinced about all that, but if I'm honest, I have to admit that I don't always have a *passionate* conviction. I believe the truth, but I haven't always experienced that truth so deeply that, in Paul's words, I am "compelled" to preach it.

And that's because of the second truth: in every sermon where people are deeply impacted, I have prayed that sermon from my head into my heart and gotten myself out of the way so the Spirit can work through me. I spend so much of my sermon preparation getting the truth out of the text, onto the page, and into my head. I desperately want to have something true and clear and relevant and interesting to say on Sunday. And I forget—or more honestly, I give short shrift to—prayer.

The result is that I get up in the pulpit to preach God's Word, but I do it in my own strength, relying on my personality, eloquence, experience, intelligence, research, and relationship with the congregation. And the sermon might be really good and receive positive response from the listeners, but it won't move them deeply, because I haven't paid attention to those words of Paul that I have often quoted in this book: "My message and my preaching were not with wise and persuasive words, but with a demonstration of the Spirit's power" (I Corinthians 2:4). That's ultimately where passion comes from—the power of the Spirit.

Passion comes when my own deep conviction is empowered by the Holy Spirit. And that requires prayer, enough prayer to get myself out of the center of the whole preaching event so the Spirit can have that place. As the old Heidelberg Catechism says, "God gives his grace and Holy Spirit only to those who pray continually and groan inwardly, asking God for these gifts and thanking him for them." In my thirty-nine years of preaching, I have experienced that again and again. And when I have, I have preached with passion. But I get busy, I get preoccupied, I get mixed up, I get caught up in myself, and I forget. That's why I'm still on the road and why I have to keep saying to myself, "Someday you'll be a good preacher."

Chapter Ten

WIFE

"A good wife who can find?"

PROVERBS 31:10

O ver the years I have enthusiastically and shamelessly answered
that proverbial question about finding a good wife with, "I can,
and I did." The story of my journey toward good preaching
would be incomplete if I didn't look at the role of my wife. In fact, it's
very likely that I wouldn't have made much progress at all without her.
As I've mentioned a couple of times, she has always been my sharpest
critic and my strongest supporter. She, more than any other human
being, has made me the preacher I am today and will be tomorrow,
when, hopefully, I become a good one.

I would like to have entitled this chapter "Family," because it was
my family as a whole that contributed immeasurably to my growth as
a preacher. But that would have broken an inviolate family rule: "Don't
talk about the kids in the pulpit." Being a preacher's kid is already a fish-
bowl existence, so I don't make it worse by trumpeting their virtues
and accomplishments or revealing their embarrassing moments or
secret foibles. I've never broken that rule, though now, with grand-
children who don't move in my ecclesiastical circles, I can at last use
delightful stories of their progress through life.

All I will say about my children's contribution to my growth as a
preacher is that they made me happy and kept me humble. In short,

they helped to keep me thoroughly human. Watching them grow up rooted me in the cycle of life that is so exhilarating and so terrifying. They gave me so much to celebrate, and they kept me on my knees. But then, isn't that true for all parents? I know it is possible for non-parents to be good preachers; I've heard some great unmarried preachers, not to mention all those celibate priests. But parenthood for me was an essential part of keeping rooted in genuine humanity and God's sufficient grace. I wouldn't be here today without them.

My wife contributed to my preaching in the same general way, only more so, because of course, we are that biblical one flesh. But she affected my preaching in more direct, more verbal ways as well. To sum it up, she was my reality check. By that I mean she loved me too much to let me think I was better or worse than I really was. When I would get puffed up with my own sense of accomplishment or by public acclaim, she would bring me back down to earth with a pithy comment. Conversely, when I was deflated by my chronic Calvinistic self-doubt or by some pointed criticism from the self-appointed watchers on the walls of Zion, or worst of all, by the utter silence of the congregation after a sermon, she would build me up with words that were like apples of gold in a setting of silver.

As I reflect back on my journey, I can think of three specific contributions she has made to my preaching. These weren't the corner-turning, new-vista-revealing comments I've talked about elsewhere. Rather, over the years her more mundane comments have provided texture, substance, color, grit, and hard reality to my sermons. Especially in the last twenty or so years, as I have settled into a mature and satisfying relationship with the LaGrave Avenue CRC, putting into practice those hard lessons I learned in the previous twenty years, she has consistently reminded me of these three things: honesty, complexity, and specificity.

Sharon is a public high school teacher. Both in poor inner-city and affluent suburban schools, she has taught troubled and struggling students as a special education teacher. Day in and day out, she has more contact with the brokenness of the world and its need for grace than I do. I work in a church, after all, where people are supposed to be nice to each other (and surprisingly, often are), where lives are allegedly redeemed (and thankfully, genuinely are). Sharon sees quite a bit more of what people call the real world than I, though we both believe that the real "real world" is the one being constantly rebuilt by God's grace all around and through us. Be that as it may, Sharon's contact with the unchurched world helps keep me honest. When I make some grand claim about how the world is, how sin acts, how grace changes people, how Christianity works in the real world, she can tell me true stories from her educational life. That keeps me honest as a preacher—not that I believe in the efficacy of the gospel any less, but that I have to be honest about how stubborn and resistant sin is and how pervasive and amazing grace is in the world. Hopefully, that keeps my preaching more honest to life and to God, who knows the real world better than any of us.

For example, I often preach the biblical claim that nothing is impossible with God, that no one is beyond the reach of God's grace, that no one is too sinful to be redeemed or too broken to be fixed. And then Sharon will tell me about a child who was a crack baby or who suffers from fetal alcohol syndrome or who was horribly abused. In spite of all subsequent parental effort, in spite of all the medical care and psychiatric counseling money can buy, in spite of all an excellent school system with expert teachers can do, this child seems too broken to be fixed. Her future seems irrevocably filled with more pain, special care, failure, and finally institutionalization of the medical or penal sort. And I have to think hard about how grace works in and with human nature. I have to be honest about how devastating sin is, which in turn makes me more honest about how absolutely necessary God's amazing grace is. Humans cannot fix humans. God's grace is our only hope. Sharon has helped me to be honest, which has helped to make sin darker and grace brighter in my preaching.

Related to honesty is complexity. We preachers like to give simple answers to life's problems because that takes much less work. It's easier to make sermons that say, "If you do A, B will happen always and immediately. If you believe this truth, here's what will result. The issues that confuse the world are really simple when you look at them through the lens of Scripture." Besides, it has been my observation that many people desperately want simple answers. It seems as though they are saying, "Life is too complicated already. Don't make my religion complicated too." As I look around the church world lately, it has struck me that the preachers who consistently preach a simple gospel are the ones with the rapidly growing churches. People are understandably looking for something simple in this diabolically complex world.

However, the reality is that life isn't simple. Neither is the Bible. Oh yes, its basic message is simple. My theological tradition used to say that the Bible is "perspicuous," so clear that even a child can understand the heart of the gospel. Thank God that's true. However, that simple central message of "Jesus and his love" is profoundly different from anything else in the world, and thus it is incomprehensible to millions of people. In addition, the rest of the Book is not at all simple, and neither is the actual living of its words in a dreadfully confused and complicated world.

By reference to the complicated problems of her students, and, on a larger scale, the complexities of the entire public education enterprise, Sharon often reminds me that "just keeping it simple" can be pretty stupid. Distinctions and nuances, problems and questions, ramifications and complications, and downright mystery are all part of the complexity of life and its redemption. A recent sermon on patience was influenced by her experience with troubled students and with prickly colleagues and frantic parents. As we talked about it, it struck me that patience takes different forms depending on whether the object of your patience is just plain wicked or deeply wounded or simply weak. My sermon on that fruit of the Spirit reflected the complexity of personal relationships because of Sharon's real-life experience with complexity. Good preaching must take account of that, while still proclaiming the simple gospel. Not an easy job. That's why I'm so glad to have this good wife God found for me.

Sharon has influenced my preaching in one more major way:

specificity. If there is one thing that irritates Sharon in a sermon, it is spiritual generalities, religious platitudes, doctrinal bromides. Broad, cliche-ridden statements might be true, but they aren't dynamic or related to real life. Her most frequent criticism in the dry times of my preaching ministry has always been, "You said a bunch of theologically true stuff that didn't catch my attention at all because I've heard it all a thousand times before. There was nothing specifically related to my life."

Over the years, Sharon has urged me to be specific. Use action verbs that create images. Paint verbal pictures with vivid metaphors and similes. Pepper your sermon with cultural allusions. Spice things up with contemporary or ancient quotations. Tell stories—not stories found in books of sermon illustrations (I have an old one from seminary days about a Kaffir man that still elicits groans from her), but stories drawn from great literature or the *New York Times* or our own daily lives. And speak to the specific situations in people's lives.

The best thing about Sharon's insistence on specificity is that she gives me all kinds of great stuff to use. While my mind is linear and logical, hers is divergent and imaginative. She sees sermon ideas and illustrations and stories and turns of phrase everywhere. I'm not ashamed to say that a good deal of the really lively material in my sermons comes from her, as her eye for the specific dimensions of sin and grace catches things I would never see or use.

I tell you these things not to brag about my wife, but to give credit where credit is due. And I want to encourage all preachers to listen to those who are closest to them, and to encourage those significant others to share the treasures of their otherness with their preachers. I haven't always listened well or responded favorably to my wife's contributions, and I'm poorer for it. Who knows? I might have become a good preacher by now if I'd just paid more attention to my wife and children.

Chapter Eleven

NEXT

"He went...even though he did not know where he was going."

<small>HEBREWS 11:8</small>

I don't know where my journey to really good preaching will take me next, what twists and turns lie ahead on the mountain road to homiletical excellence. But I've been at this too long and experienced too many perspective shifts to think there's nothing left to learn. As I've often said, whenever I think I've arrived, God has something else to teach me about preaching, often from the mouths of some nonprofessional critics. So who knows where the road leads next?

I do know that I see several giant boulders in the road just ahead, great challenges that may well result in another of those significant shifts in perspective. The first has to do with that ubiquitous philosophy called postmodernism. Claiming that all truth is relative, postmodernism directly challenges the absolute truth claims of the Christian faith with the mantra, "That's just your truth."

PREACHING TO POSTMODERNS

While my congregation is probably more premodern ("God is truth") or modern (with a deep reverence for science), there is enough postmodernism in them to challenge me. When I suggested to my tenth-grade catechism class that the second commandment might have something negative to say about non-Christian religions, some of them indignantly protested that all religions are true. "That's their truth. Jesus is our truth." And quite apart from present church members, we're going to encounter the pervasive relativism of postmodernism more and more as we reach out to unchurched folk. Will we need to preach differently to postmoderns? And if so, how?

In an effort to address that question, I recently led an eight-month seminar with new church planters working for CRC Home Missions. Under the auspices of the Center for Excellence in Preaching at Calvin Seminary, I wanted to explore with these frontline warriors whether and how the centuries-old Heidelberg Catechism might be helpful in preaching to postmoderns. CRC ministers are expected to use that pastorally warm and Christ-centered confession as a guide for preaching in one service every Sunday. It was my hunch (proven to be correct) that these new church planters didn't do that. Many established church preachers don't either. Acknowledging that such a project might seem counterintuitive, I encouraged them to find ways in which the approach of the Catechism paralleled or dovetailed with some of the unique features of postmodernism. For example, though postmoderns are generally hostile to organized religion, they are frequently quite open to hearing about genuine Christianity, of which they are often woefully ignorant. I suggested that the Catechism's outline of Christian truth (which pretty much parallels the sin-salvation-service outline of Paul's Epistle to the Romans) is a valuable sermon guide for missionary preaching to postmodern seekers.

We discovered other connecting points between the Catechism and postmodernism that present unique challenges to preachers of the Bible. For example, though postmoderns tend to be antiauthoritarian, they do have respect for other people's traditions. After all, your tradition is your truth. Theoretically, it should be perfectly legitimate to preach the gospel as understood in your own tradition, in my case, in the Heidelberg Catechism. "However," say some students of postmodernism, "you must do so in a non-dogmatic way." Dogmatism, says Graham Johnston in his *Preaching to a Postmodern World,* is "the kiss of death" with postmodern folks. So how do I preach the Reformed version of the Christian faith which I believe is really (not just relatively) true without being dogmatic?

Or again, postmodern thinkers have a love of mystery, of the numinous, the transcendent; so if I'm going to address them, my sermons must acknowledge the deep mystery of God, of grace, of salvation. That's not hard to do, since mystery is a key concept particularly in Paul, and paradox is a major theological idea in my high Calvinistic tradition. But I don't believe that mystery means there are no absolutes, no final answers. Mystery is part of the Christian faith, but not the whole of it. How does the preacher acknowledge that there is mystery in the Christian faith while still insisting that the Bible is God's revelation of the truth?

I don't have the answers to these kinds of questions. And I'm more than a little concerned that the next decade may be so filled with discussions about the problems presented by postmodernism that we forget to straightforwardly preach the old story that the Holy Spirit has used to convert people of all philosophical stripes across the centuries. But I don't think my confidence in the power of the Holy Spirit and my love for the simple gospel story mean I can stop thinking about the implications of postmodernism for my preaching.

PREACHING TO YOUTH

Another challenge for me lies in the area of preaching to teens and young adults. Pollsters like George Barna tell us that literally millions of youth are simply lost to the church. When they leave high school and the authority of the parental home, they drop out of church, and many never return. Christian Smith, in *Soul Searching,* his monumental study of youth religion, discovered that even churched teens are remarkably inarticulate about their "Christian" faith, most of them holding to something Smith calls "moralistic therapeutic deism." God wants you to be good and he's there to help when you need it. But most of the time, God is as distant from the lives of young people as deism's venerable watchmaker.

As I said in my reflections on passion, LaGrave Church recently received a grant from the Calvin Institute of Christian Worship that enabled us to study how a church with traditional worship like ours can involve teens in the life of the church and in lifelong Christian discipleship. Because of the current widespread notion that a church has to offer contemporary worship to attract and hold teens, we were prepared to hear our own kids say that they wanted a new musical style at LaGrave. Some did say that, but interestingly, and alarmingly to me, what they talked about most was preaching. They didn't care about worship style nearly as much as preaching. Not only were they looking for passion in the preacher, but they also insisted on sermons addressed to their specific concerns as young people. Much of our wider research revealed the same thing.

Wanting personally relevant sermons is nothing new, but there is a unique challenge for this sixty-something preacher in the pleas of my own teenage members. And it's not just a challenge for an old guy like me. All preachers must wrestle with the issue of how to meaningfully address a whole generation accustomed to getting its information via electronic media. That media absolutely engulfs them in a world I do not understand. Back when my children were that age, I was in touch with popular youth culture. Not anymore. And it's not enough to simply say (as preachers did when I was young), "Now I want to say a word to you young people." I've discovered that such a direct appeal usually results in averted eyes, slumped shoulders, and the unmistakable sound of defense mechanisms rolling into place. To preach to teens, I have to speak their language (without saying "Dude") and address their unique concerns using references from their own culture.

Let me tell you how personal and painful this has become for me. A recent e-mail from the eleventh- and twelve-grade church school class critiqued my sermons in a way that may well produce the next big turn on my mountain highway. This missive, by the way, was not gratuitous. In response to our study on worship and youth, this class aimed to help our youth understand our worship. They came to the subject of preaching, and following what I am told was a spirited discussion, they sent me a detailed critique of my sermons. "Your exposition [yes, they used that word] of the Word is interesting and helpful," they said, "but your application to our lives is so general that we don't have any idea what to do after a sermon is done." They went on to suggest very specific ways I might have applied several recent sermons.

I have to tell you that I was stunned and (not surprisingly) more than a little defensive. I mean, these were sermons that had been hugely appreciated by the congregation, at least from the folks who took the time to comment. Now these kids were telling me that these sermons might have been true and interesting, but they missed the mark in their lives. What was wrong with these upstarts? Why couldn't they apply the truth themselves? Did I have to spoon-feed them? Did I have to do that with every age group, and all in twenty minutes?

When I recovered from my spasm of defensiveness and was able to think clearly, I was able to communicate a couple of concerns to that class by e-mail, followed by an extended dialogue at their next class session. I told them that I had two major convictions about this whole business of application. The first goes all the way back to seminary days, when someone (I don't know if it was my homiletics professor) said that we shouldn't make specific applications. That, said this person, is the work of the Holy Spirit. There is no way you can capture all of the ways in which a text will relate to the individual lives of all those people in front of you, so you shouldn't even try. Make the sermon generally applicable, which means that it should address a real human need, one of the universal ones. Then let the Spirit lead each congregant into the specific application of that truth for that life. Perhaps because of that early homiletical advice, I've rarely aimed a sermon at the specific need of one person or one age group. Now these teenagers were saying that if I didn't, they would find my sermons irrelevant, and thus boring.

The other conviction that was jostled by their missive is of more recent vintage. Having studied and then co-taught a class at Calvin Seminary using Paul Scott Wilson's *The Four Pages of the Sermon,* I really believe that a sermon should end on a note of grace. Though I've expressed my questions about this in chapter eight, Wilson has challenged me to make grace central to my preaching. Grace, he says, must

be not only central, but also terminal, not only the climax but also the
end point of every sermon. After plumbing the depths of human
trouble in the text and in contemporary life, the preacher should lift
people up with the message of God's amazing grace. People should
leave the service with the Good News on their minds and hearts. They
don't need six points of application, a checklist of the things they must
do now. Wilson suggests that such a homiletical approach turns the
gospel into law at the last moment. Leave rejoicing in what God has
done, not laboring under the burden of what you must now do in
response to God's grace.

Now these kids were saying, "Tell us what to do, and be specific
about it." I've had adults say similar things. Are they all missing the
point of grace? Or does Wilson's way of preaching miss something
important in the task? Or, more likely, am I missing something in both
the critique of these young people and the expert advice of that master preacher? How does one specifically apply the message of God's
grace in Christ without introducing a checklist of things to do that
effectively blots out grace?

My communication with that class was actually quite helpful. They
heard and understood my concerns, even expressing appreciation for
the difficulty of preaching to a large intergenerational church. And they
helped me think about this whole new area of preaching. I don't have
clear resolution yet, but they stimulated me tremendously.

As with all the great turns on my journey, I can't say that I'm com-
fortable with this new problem and its accompanying new perspective. But somehow this sixty-something preacher must find a way to
address young people without sounding ridiculous or patronizing and
without alienating the rest of the congregation in the process. Of course,
there's a sense in which the supposedly unique problems of youth are
universal problems. But I heard that class say they need to hear universal problems addressed in a way that will help them hear and believe
and live the gospel.

I must also take great care that my preaching to youth is prophetic
as well as pastoral. I can't simply enter into their youth world uncriti-

cally for the sake of building a communication bridge, because certain features of youth culture should come under the judgment of the gospel. Addiction to the computer, fascination with the lifestyles of some popular artists, an overly tolerant attitude to the sex and violence that permeates some genres of entertainment, the adoption of the relativistic morality of postmodernism—all these are a great hindrance to faith and life. That must be said, lovingly but clearly. So perhaps I shall spend the rest of my preaching ministry learning to preach to young people while not losing the older folks or selling out the gospel.

Preaching to the Marginalized

Finally, I find myself challenged by something at the very edge of the road. In fact, I wouldn't even be aware of this except for the comment of a good friend. I had preached what I thought was a really helpful sermon on marriage and parenting. But the next day my friend, with an almost mournful look, said, "I wonder how my daughter would have heard that sermon." His daughter is a marvelous woman who struggles with life as a single mother of two. I had to confess that I hadn't even thought of someone like her when I preached that sermon. I was thinking of the vast center, of people like me—not people like her, at the margins.

My friend's daughter isn't nearly as close to the margins of society as others at LaGrave. She has a job, a home, a family, a church. Recently, we have seen a significant influx of homeless folks from the mean streets of the Heartside District. As I hinted earlier, LaGrave is located in an area that in former days would have been called Skid Row. Though it is now being renovated at a breathtaking pace, there are still 1500 or so of these poor folks at our very doorstep. For years LaGrave has offered a wide variety of ministry services to these often mentally ill, drug-addicted, jobless, homeless people. Now, however, some of them are actually worshiping with us and even becoming members. I used to preach *about* them, urging my affluent congregation to be involved in Christ's ministry of compassion and justice to the poor. Now I have to think about how to preach *among* them, as the marginalized of our society are sitting right next to us.

For years I've heard about reading the Bible from the margins, reading it through the eyes of the oppressed. Reading the stories about violence toward women from the perspective of those women, for example, gives a very different sense to those texts. I've always found such marginalized reading fascinating, though I've sometimes been troubled by the way the central message of the gospel can get sidelined in such interpretations. The gospel sometimes ends up being about human problems and human rights, rather than about what God did to solve those problems when he sent his Son to bring the kingdom of God to earth. As I learn to pay attention to those at the margins of my congregation and our society, I need to be careful that what I bring them is the good news of the Triune God who calls all kinds of people to repentance and faith in Christ so they can find new life at the center of his loving kingdom.

Those are some of the things I'm wrestling with now as I continue the journey. I don't know exactly what to do with them at the moment. And I surely don't know if any one of them—or all of them—will lead to the next great turn in the road. That's why I'm so glad that God has the last word in all this.

Chapter Twelve

SPIRIT

"He will lead you into all the truth."

JOHN 16:13

B efore closing this book, I must say a word about that last word—*Spirit,* as in the Holy Spirit. When I've said all I have to say about my long and serpentine journey toward becoming a good preacher, I find myself returning once again to those ringing words of Paul in I Corinthians 2:4–5: "My message and my preaching were not with wise and persuasive words, but with a demonstration of the Spirit's power, so that your faith might not rest on man's wisdom, but on God's power."

If you read Paul's letters or his sermons in Acts, you will find a highly educated, worldly-wise, and verbally eloquent preacher. Every preacher should strive to develop and grow as much as humanly possible, because God always works incarnationally, through the gifts and experiences of real people. But Paul knew that the real power in preaching, the power that not only informs and entertains and motivates, but actually brings people to saving faith in Jesus Christ, comes from the Holy Spirit. That is my ultimate source of confidence whenever I mount the pulpit and as I continue this journey toward being a good preacher someday. "The Holy Spirit will lead [me] into all the truth" (John 16:13).

I didn't pay much attention to the Spirit when I began this journey, except as a small part of Christian doctrine. (We didn't have a course in pneumatology at Calvin Theological Seminary then.) Besides, I didn't need the Spirit. No, I didn't consciously think that, but the fact was that I never really thought about the Spirit. After all, I had been called by God to this, and God had gifted me with intelligence and eloquence (just ask me). I had received one of the finest educations available. I had all I needed, except, obviously, humility.

My humbling began very early in St. Louis, however, and I soon found myself desperate, not just because of the constant coaching by the Monday-morning quarterbacks I talked about back in chapter two, but also because of homiletical crop failure. The theologically correct sermons that satisfied the truth police didn't seem to be growing that little mission church. I became increasingly upset about that lack of growth as two neighboring churches, one Baptist and the other charismatic, were growing like the church in Acts.

In fact, I became so desperate about the situation that I finally listened to the more charismatic members of my church who had been chanting the same words in my ears for some time, like a kind of Pentecostal mantra: "The Holy Spirit. The Holy Spirit. The Holy Spirit. You need the Holy Spirit."

"But I have the Holy Spirit," I replied in good Reformed fashion. "Every Christian does."

"Ah," they would say with infuriatingly knowing smiles, "but you need to be baptized in the Spirit. You need to be anointed with the Spirit. You need to consciously receive the Holy Spirit."

Under the duress of failure, these and other turns of phrase about the ministry of the Holy Spirit finally penetrated my hard head and harder heart and awakened me to my need for the Spirit in my work of preaching, not to mention in my own sanctification.

Over the years I have had to learn that lesson over and over again. And I've pursued a number of (sometimes strange) disciplines to open myself to the work of the Spirit. In Colorado Springs, for example, I would intentionally and foolishly stay up very late on Saturday night watching ridiculous old movies so that I would be exhausted on Sunday morning. That way, I reasoned, I wouldn't be able to rely on my own strength; I would have to rely on the Spirit's power. When I shared my secret with a visiting pastor, he looked at me like I had lost my young mind and said simply, "That's very interesting." (Of course, what he meant was, "This young fool is in serious trouble.") Now I go to bed very early on Saturday night so I'll be physically rested for the arduous task of preaching, but I only go to bed after praying for a very long time that the Spirit will work through me and in the congregation the next day.

LIGHT AND POWER

Years ago in Denver, Colorado, there was a charismatic Episcopalian church near my childhood home that called itself "The Holy Spirit Light and Power Company." That's how I think about the Holy Spirit in relation to preaching. He's the source of light and power. When I begin to work on a sermon, I ask the Spirit to enlighten me, to lead me to the truth, to give me ideas, to make connections, to guide my research, to bring something creatively redemptive out of the chaos of words and ideas. Then I write it all out on my computer. Some preachers wait for the Spirit to give them light in the pulpit. They do some study during the week, think about what they want to say in general, and then pray a lot that the Spirit will guide them on Sunday morning. Apart from the fact that my performance anxiety would never let me do that, I also think that such preparation comes perilously close to testing God in a negative way. I think that God wants us to study his Word and the culture really hard, think about the sermon very clearly, and choose words with great care, thus preaching the truth as clearly and interestingly and pointedly as humanly possible. So I ask the Holy Spirit for light in my study.

Then I ask for power for the pulpit. My prayer is always that the power of the Spirit will perform the miracle of homiletical transubstantiation. I ask the Spirit to take my ordinary human words, those carefully prepared black marks on my six computer-generated pages, and transform them into the very Word of God to his people. Without the Spirit's power, I will not be persuasive, compassionate, authoritative, humble, loving, daring, or anything else I need to be as a preacher of the gospel. I may have the most beautiful and persuasive biblical sermon I've ever made, but without the Spirit's power, it will not become the life-changing Word of God. And without the Spirit's power, people's minds will not be open, their hearts will not be soft, their wills will not be malleable, and their emotions will not be stirred. I pray that in the moment of preaching, the power of the Spirit will shake the whole place and everyone in it so that the Word of God will have its full effect. No amount of *me* will make it happen. It's the work of the Spirit.

It's no surprise that the record of the early church in the book of Acts, that amazing story of numerical, geographical, and spiritual growth, is often called "the Acts of the Holy Spirit." Again and again, the apostles and others preached their hearts out, drawing on everything they had learned thus far on their journey. But it was the Mighty Wind of God who used those preachers to fan the flame of the gospel into a blessed conflagration that raced to the ends of the earth in a few short years. That's what I want for my preaching.

The Holy Spirit has been the ultimate source of all the growth I've experienced as a preacher. Though God always used the words of people, it was the Spirit who made those words shine like xenon headlights on my homiletical journey. More importantly, it was the Spirit's power that moved me to change. Apart from the Spirit, I'd still be way back somewhere, bound to what I thought was good preaching. I don't think Paul was focusing on preachers when he wrote II Corinthians 3:17–18. But his words summarize my experience and anchor my hope for the rest of the journey: "Now the Lord is the Spirit, and where the Spirit of the Lord is, there is freedom. And we, who with unveiled faces all reflect the Lord's glory, are being transformed into his likeness with ever-increasing glory [or as my favorite translation says, "we are being changed from one degree of glory to another"], which comes from the Lord, who is the Spirit."

Because of the light and power of the Holy Spirit, I still have hope that someday I'll be a good preacher. I have the same hope for you, if you stay on the road—neither settling into the way you've always done things nor setting your heels against criticisms and suggestions from foe or friend, but letting the Spirit use all those words to change you from one degree of glory to another. Trust him. He will lead you into all the truth. And someday you'll be a good preacher.

AFTERWORD

That is my very petite narrative, my pilgrimage as a preacher in the little Dutch Reformed subculture. Clearly, it is not a prescription for all who preach. But it is a description of the mountain road I have been traveling for almost forty years now. If you're looking for something bigger than that, a metanarrative on preaching, may I suggest that you study the Gospels, where the great Teacher and Preacher shows us definitively how to do it. As the Word made flesh, the incarnation of all God has to say to the human race, Jesus was the most effective preacher ever to stand on a mountainside or sit in a boat. That is why I take great comfort in the fact that of the thousands who cried, "What a great preacher!" only twelve of his listeners "got it" well enough to pass it on to others. And that was after three years of the best seminary education ever offered, and of course, the Resurrection.

If you are looking for a great preacher, one who has truly arrived, study Jesus. You'll find the message ("The kingdom is near, so believe the Good News, repent, and follow me") and the method (stories, stories, stories, along with proverbs and prophecies, diatribes and sheer didactic).

Or study the Apostle Paul. More than anyone else, it was Paul who brought the gospel to the world with his passionate, uncompromising, biblical, theological, and practical sermons. That's why I take great comfort in the fact that Paul didn't think he was much of a preacher, at least compared to the great orators of his day who spoke with "wise and persuasive words" (I Corinthians 2:4). His critics agreed completely that he wasn't much in the pulpit: "His letters are weighty and forceful, but in person he is unimpressive and his speaking amounts to nothing" (II Corinthians 10:10).

You'll find metanarrative enough in the Scripture in the examples of Christ and his most influential disciple. I offer you only my own story. I don't feel bad about that, because I've always found it helpful to read the stories of practicing preachers—whether fictional or real. It was the old-fashioned story of the *Rev. Andrew Connington* by Grace Irwin that moved me to enter a more personal relationship with God after I had been in ministry for a year. Anyone who has read *Gilead,* Marilynn Robinson's Pulitzer Prize-winning novel, has been moved by her insights into the life of a preacher. And if you haven't read Richard Lischer's *Open Secrets* or Jeff Berryman's *Leaving Ruin* or the classic *Diary of a Country Priest* by George Bernanos, you have many pages of reading delight and personal growth ahead of you. These slice-of-life portraits have enriched my preaching life a great deal.

I hope that this slice of *my* life has enriched yours at least a little. Thanks for traveling with me. May God bless you as you get on the road again, whether you are one of those listeners who help preachers see new vistas or one of the thousands of preachers who keep on trucking until the day the critics stop saying, "Someday you'll be a good preacher."

ENDNOTES

1. Lynn Freed, *Reading, Writing, and Leaving Home,* quoted in *The Christian Century,* Vol. 123, No. 4, February 21, 2006, p. 6.

2. Anthony Robinson, *Cloud of Witnesses: An Audio Journal on Youth, Church and Culture,* Vol. 9, Princeton Theological Seminary Institute for Youth Ministry, quoted in *The Christian Century,* Vol. 123, No. 4, February 21, 2006, p. 6.

3. Eugene Petersen, *Eat This Book,* Wm. B. Eerdman Publishing Company, Grand Rapids, MI, 2006, p. 59.